Ecce Romani

A Latin Reading Program
Revised Edition

4

W9-CZH-996

Pastimes
and Ceremonies

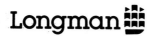
Longman

Ecce Romani Student's Book 4 Pastimes and Ceremonies

First Printing 1985
5 4 3 2

ISBN 0 582 36667 4

Illustrated by Trevor Parkin and Claudia Sargent. Cover illustration by Judy Hans Price.

This edition of *Ecce Romani* is based on *Ecce Romani: A Latin Reading Course*, originally prepared by The Scottish Classics Group © copyright The Scottish Classics Group 1971, 1982, and published in the United Kingdom by Oliver and Boyd, a Division of Longman Group. This edition has been prepared by a team of American and Canadian educators:

Authors: Professor Gilbert Lawall, University of Massachusetts, Amherst, Massachusetts

David Tafe, Rye Country Day School, Rye, New York

Consultants: Dr. Rudolph Masciantonio, Philadelphia Public Schools, Pennsylvania

Ronald Palma, Holland Hall School, Tulsa, Oklahoma

Dr. Edward Barnes, C. W. Jefferys Secondary School, Downsview, Ontario

Shirley Lowe, Wayland Public Schools, Wayland, Massachusetts

Longman Inc.
95 Church Street
White Plains, N.Y. 10601
Distributed in Canada by Academic Press Ltd., 55 Barber Greene Road, Don Mills, Ontario MC3 2A1, Canada.

Printed in the U.S.A.

CONTENTS

41
At the Baths

One of the main entertainments of the Roman was his daily visit to the baths—either to the public **thermae** or to the smaller, private **balneae**. He would expect to find three basic rooms: a warm room (**tepidārium**) which he would enter after undressing in the changing-room (**apodytērium**); a hot room (**caldārium**) where hot water would be provided in a specially heated room which might also incorporate a steam bath; and a cold room (**frīgidārium**) where he could plunge into a cold bath after the heat of the caldārium. To clean himself, the Roman would have himself rubbed down with oil (**unguentum**) which was then scraped off with a special metal instrument (**strigilis**). He would also expect to find an exercise ground (**palaestra**), often in the open air, with a covered portico around it, where he could take exercise by playing with a ball (**pilā lūdere**), by wrestling (**luctārī**), by fencing at a post (**pālus**), or by weightlifting. There was a great variety of ball games including **harpastum**, a game involving the "snatching" (**rapere**) of a heavy ball, and **trigōn**, a throwing and catching game played by three people. At the end of it all he would be rubbed down with a towel (**linteum**). The baths were regarded as a social club, and people went there to exercise, play games, and meet each other, as well as to wash.

Iam hōra sexta erat. Titus Cornēlius, ut cōtīdiē solēbat, domō ēgressus, in Campum Martium ad Thermās Nerōnēās dēscendit, nam eō amīcī eius conveniēbant et dē rēbus urbānīs colloquēbantur.

Quō cum Titus pervēnisset, pecūniā datā, in vestibulum ingressus est. Ibi complūrēs ex amīcīs eum salūtāvērunt atque ūnā in apodytērium iniērunt. Vestīmenta exūta trādidērunt servīs suīs, quī unguenta et strigilēs portābant. 5

Iam ūnctī in palaestram exiērunt ubi multī cīvēs variīs modīs sē exercēbant. Aliī harpastum rapiēbant, aliī trigōne lūdēbant, aliī luctābantur, aliī pālum gladiō petēbant. Titus cum duōbus amīcīs trigōne lūdēbat. Cum 10 satis sē ita exercuissent, ā servīs plūs unguentī poposcērunt et strigilibus dēfrictī sunt. Mox tepidārium, deinde caldārium iniērunt. Hīc, cum calōrem et vapōrem vix patī possent, haud multum morābantur. Cum in tepidārium regressī essent, statim inde frīgidārium intrāvērunt et in aquam frīgidam dēsiluērunt. Posteā linteīs tersī, vestīmenta rūrsus induērunt. 15

7

Nē tum quidem domum discessērunt sed, vīnō sūmptō, inter sē colloquī coepērunt. Titum, cum ille semper vidērētur omnia audīvisse et vīdisse, dē rēbus urbānīs omnēs rogābant. Maximē enim cupiēbant cognōscere quid in senātū agerētur, cūr prīnceps ipse senātōrēs omnēs Rōmam arcessīvisset, quae scelera lībertī Caesaris admitterent. 20

"Nīl novī," respondit Titus, "sed heri in Balneīs Palātīnīs rem rīdiculam vīdī; senex calvus, tunicā russātā indūtus, inter puerōs capillātōs pilā lūdēbat. Eās pilās, quae ad terram ceciderant, nōn repetēbat, nam servus follem habēbat plēnum pilārum quās lūdentibus dabat. Tandem hic senex digitōs concrepuit et aquam poposcit. Tum, cum manūs lāvisset, in capite ūnīus 25 ē puerīs tersit!"

Campus Martius, the Plain of Mars on the outskirts of Rome
Nerōnēus, -a, -um, of Nero
quō cum, when . . . there
pecūniā datā, after paying his entrance fee
vestibulum, -ī (n), entrance passage
vestīmenta, -ōrum (n pl), clothes
exerceō (2), to exercise, train
calor, calōris (m), heat

haud, not
posteā, afterwards
vīnō sūmptō, after a drink of wine
scelus, sceleris (n), crime
senex, senis (m), old man
calvus, -a, -um, bald
capillātus, -a, -um, with long hair
follis, follis (m), bag
digitus, -ī (m), finger

exuō, exuere (3), exuī, exūtum, to take off
unguō, unguere (3), ūnxī, ūnctum, to anoint, smear with oil
dēfricō, dēfricāre (1), dēfricuī, dēfrictum, to rub down
tergeō, tergēre (2), tersī, tersum, to dry, wipe
cognōscō, cognōscere (3), cognōvī, cognitum, to find out, learn
admittō, admittere (3), admīsī, admissum, to commit (a crime)
repetō, repetere (3), repetīvī, repetītum, to pick up, recover
concrepō, concrepāre (1), concrepuī, to snap (the fingers)

Exercise 41a

Using story 41 as a guide, give the Latin for:

1. When Titus had arrived there, several of his friends greeted him.
2. When they had exercised enough, they entered the warm room.
3. Since they were scarcely able to endure the heat of the hot room, they returned to the warm room.
4. Since Titus seemed to know everything, they asked him about affairs of the town.
5. They wanted to learn why the Emperor had summoned the senators to Rome and what the senators were doing in the senate.

A bronze oil flask and two strigils. (Reproduced
by courtesy of the Trustees of the British Museum)

VERBS: Subjunctive Mood I

Look at these sentences:

Pīrātae rogābant quī **essēmus**, unde **vēnissēmus**, quō iter **facerēmus**.
*The pirates kept asking who we were, where we had come from, and
where we were traveling.*

Cum sē **exercuissent**, in tepidārium ingressī sunt.
When they had exercised, they went into the warm room.

Grammaticus tamen, cum ego **ignōrārem**, ferulam rapuit et mē crūdē-
lissimē verberāvit.
*The teacher, however, since I didn't know, snatched his cane and beat
me very cruelly.*

Cum nāvis in īnsulam ventīs **acta esset**, nōs in terram ēvāsimus.
*When the ship had been driven on to the island by the winds, we escaped
ashore.*

The verbs in bold type are examples of the *subjunctive mood* which frequently occurs in Latin in subordinate clauses.

9

Imperfect Subjunctive

This tense of the subjunctive is formed from the present active infinitive by the addition of the personal endings:

	esse
S 1	esse*m*
S 2	essē*s*
S 3	esse*t*
P 1	essē*mus*
P 2	essē*tis*
P 3	esse*nt*

So also the irregular verbs **posse, velle, nōlle, īre,** and **ferre.**

ACTIVE VOICE				
	1st Conjugation	*2nd Conjugation*	*3rd Conjugation*		*4th Conjugation*
S 1	portāre*m*	movēre*m*	mittere*m*	iacere*m*	audīre*m*
S 2	portārē*s*	movērē*s*	mitterē*s*	iacerē*s*	audīrē*s*
S 3	portāre*t*	movēre*t*	mittere*t*	iacere*t*	audīre*t*
P 1	portārē*mus*	movērē*mus*	mitterē*mus*	iacerē*mus*	audīrē*mus*
P 2	portārē*tis*	movērē*tis*	mitterē*tis*	iacerē*tis*	audīrē*tis*
P 3	portāre*nt*	movēre*nt*	mittere*nt*	iacere*nt*	audīre*nt*

PASSIVE VOICE				
S 1	portāre*r*	movēre*r*	mittere*r*	iacere*r*	audīre*r*
S 2	portārē*ris*	movērē*ris*	mitterē*ris*	iacerē*ris*	audīrē*ris*
S 3	portārē*tur*	movērē*tur*	mitterē*tur*	iacerē*tur*	audīrē*tur*
P 1	portārē*mur*	movērē*mur*	mitterē*mur*	iacerē*mur*	audīrē*mur*
P 2	portārē*minī*	movērē*minī*	mitterē*minī*	iacerē*minī*	audīrē*minī*
P 3	portāre*ntur*	movēre*ntur*	mittere*ntur*	iacere*ntur*	audīre*ntur*

DEPONENT VERBS				
S 1	cōnāre*r* etc.	verēre*r* etc.	loquere*r* etc.	regredere*r* etc.	experīre*r* etc.

10

Note in the 1st person singular sample of deponent verbs given above that deponents form the imperfect subjunctive by adding the passive endings to a form that would be the *active infinitive* if deponent verbs had an active infinitive, thus cōnāre- + -r = cōnārer.

Pluperfect Subjunctive

The *active* of all verbs is made up of the perfect active infinitive plus the personal endings.

The *passive* is made up in the same way as the indicative passive (see Chapter 30), but essem is substituted for eram.

	ACTIVE VOICE	PASSIVE VOICE		DEPONENT	
1	audīvissem	audītus, -a	essem	cōnātus, -a	essem
S 2	audīvissēs	audītus, -a	essēs	cōnātus, -a	essēs
3	audīvisset	audītus, -a, -um	esset	cōnātus, -a, -um	esset
1	audīvissēmus	audītī, -ae	essēmus	cōnātī, -ae	essēmus
P 2	audīvissētis	audītī, -ae	essētis	cōnātī, -ae	essētis
3	audīvissent	audītī, -ae, -a	essent	cōnātī, -ae, -a	essent

Be sure to learn all of the subjunctive forms above thoroughly.

Some Uses of the Subjunctive: Circumstantial and Causal Clauses and Indirect Questions

The examples of the subjunctive you have met so far have been in subordinate clauses beginning with cum ("when," "since") or a question word. When cum means "when," its clause describes the *circumstances* in which the action of the main clause took place. When cum means "since," its clause describes the *cause* or the reason why the action of the main clause took place. When the subordinate clause begins with a question word, the clause is said to express an *indirect question*.

In all of these clauses the subjunctive is translated into English as the corresponding tense of the indicative. The imperfect subjunctive indicates an action going on at the *same time* as that of the main verb of the sentence. Translate with ". . . was . . ." or ". . . were . . . ," e.g.:

Pīrātae rogābant quō iter facerēmus.
The pirates were asking where we **were** *traveling.*

The pluperfect subjunctive expresses an action that took place *before* that of the main verb. Translate with ". . . had . . . ," e.g.:

Pīrātae rogābant unde vēnissēmus.
The pirates were asking where we **had** *come from.*

11

Exercise 41b

In the Latin sentences on page 9 under VERBS: Subjunctive Mood I, locate two circumstantial clauses, one causal clause, and three indirect questions.

Exercise 41c

Read aloud and translate each sentence, and then identify each subordinate clause by type (circumstantial, causal, indirect question). Comment on the temporal relationship between the actions of the subordinate clauses and those of the main clauses.

1. Pīrātae rogābant quis esset meus dominus et quō īret.
2. Cum nōllem dominum relinquere, cōnātus sum eum servāre.
3. Cum prīmā lūce profectī essēmus, iam dēfessī erāmus.
4. Lūdī magister rogāvit unde Aenēās vēnisset et quō nāvigāre in animō habēret.
5. Cum multōs annōs nāvigāvissēmus, tandem ad Italiam pervēnimus.
6. Grammaticus mē rogāvit quandō domō abiissem.
7. Māter fīlium rogāvit cūr īrātus esset.
8. Cum diū ambulāvissent, dēfessī erant.
9. Cum lupum cōnspexissem, quam celerrimē aufūgī.
10. Ego nesciēbam cūr Rōmam proficīscerēmur.

The women's changing-room (**apodytērium**) of the baths at Herculaneum. (Photograph: the Mansell Collection)

The Baths

In addition to the many references to baths in Roman literature, much information about the **balneae** and **thermae** can be deduced from the archaeological remains of bathing establishments still evident today. In Rome, the great Thermae of Diocletian now house the National Museum, its extensive grounds having been laid out by Michelangelo centuries after the baths were built. Grand opera is performed during the summer months in the Baths of Caracalla.

At Pompeii, both public and private bathing establishments have been found, and even in many of the houses there are full suites of bathrooms— warm, hot, and cold rooms—which were apparently used only by the family. On country estates and in town houses, in addition to the suites of baths for the owner, there were bath houses for slaves.

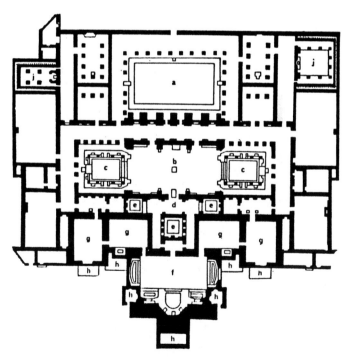

Hadrian's Baths at Lepcis Magna (A.D. 126-7). Open-air swimming-bath (*a*), **frīgidārium** (*b*), plunge-baths (*c*), **tepidārium** (*d*), with a large central and two smaller baths (*e*), **caldārium** (*f*), super-heated rooms (*g*), furnaces (*h*), and latrines (*j*).

The first public baths in Rome were built in the second century B.C.; they were small, practical wash-houses for men only. Later, bathing establishments called **balneae** began to be built at private expense and run for profit by individuals or a consortium. As the practice of bathing became more and more popular, huge baths (**thermae**) were built by the state. These were increased in size and splendor under the emperors, e.g., the Thermae of Caracalla (A.D. 217) and of Diocletian (A.D. 303).

Romans of all social classes could spend an hour or more in the luxury of such complexes for only a **quadrāns**, the smallest Roman coin. Children were admitted free. The management of the state **thermae** was awarded for a fixed sum to a contractor. Sometimes a rich citizen or magistrate undertook to pay him the equivalent of the total entrance fees for a certain period, during which entry to the baths was entirely free.

So attached were the Romans to their daily hot steam-bath that they built baths in most communities throughout their Empire. Where there were hot springs, as in Bath, England, they used these and built gymnasia and dressing-rooms around them. Where there were no hot springs, they heated the air by "hypocausts," a system whereby hot air from a furnace circulated under the raised floor and through ducts and vents in the walls. The fuel for the furnace, which was stoked by slaves, was wood and charcoal. Huge reservoirs were built near the baths to provide a constant and plentiful supply of water.

In Rome, the baths opened at noon and remained open till dusk. The opening and closing times were indicated by the striking of a gong.

Many establishments had separate facilities for men and women bathers; others fixed different hours for the two sexes. Mixed bathing, however, was usual in the open-air swimming pools that formed part of the larger baths. Ladies who cared for their reputation did not frequent the baths.

Bathers would take various articles with them to the baths, including towels, bottles of oil, and strigils. All but the poor would bring their own slaves to attend them, but it was possible to hire the services of others at the baths (e.g., masseur, barber). Attendants would guard clothes for a small fee.

Roman baths varied considerably in size and layout, but in all of them the following series of rooms was to be found:

1. **apodytērium**: a changing room with stone benches and rows of deep holes in the walls for holding clothes.

2. **frīgidārium**: cold room, with cold plunge bath at one side.

3. **tepidārium**: warm room, to acclimatize bathers to the difference in temperature between the cold and hot rooms.

4. **caldārium**: hot room, with hot bath and hot air like the modern Turkish bath. It was the best-lit room and was equipped with basins and tubs. Its ceiling was usually domed to allow condensation to run off.

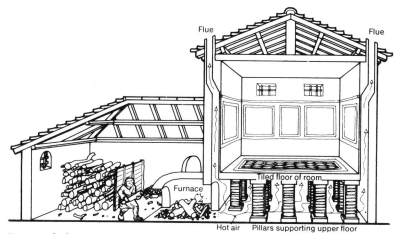

Diagram of a hypocaust

In addition, some baths had a "Spartan" room (**Lacōnicum**), where people sweated in dry heat as in a sauna. It had a dome on top with a round opening closed by a bronze disc on a chain. The bather could thus regulate the heat himself.

Remains of the Baths of Caracalla

15

The bathers could take the three stages of bathing in any order, but it was usual to end up with a cold plunge. Medicinal and perfumed baths were also available. The baths became a suitable place for taking exercise. A large complex would have a court for ball games and an area for gymnastics and wrestling, in addition to the swimming pool. There were various ball games, each using a different type of ball and sometimes a racquet as well. Hoops or a dumbbell were also used for exercising.

The Roman baths were centers for recreation and relaxation in the fullest sense, and in the largest establishments the amenities could include gardens, reading-rooms, and even libraries. "Snack-bars" (**popīnae**) were numerous inside the building or near by, while vendors of every type advertised their wares on all sides.

A Graffito from the Baths at Rome

Balnea, vīna, Venus corrumpunt corpora nostra; at vītam faciunt—balnea, vīna, Venus.

balnea = balneae	**Venus** = amor

corrumpō, corrumpere (3), corrūpī, corruptum, to spoil, harm, ruin

42
Stop Thief!

Marcus et Sextus ē lūdō ēgressī ūnā cum Eucleide et alterō servō domum
ībant. Subitō Eucleidēs puerīs, "Vultisne ad thermās īre?" inquit.
Quibus verbīs audītīs, puerī maximē gaudēbant.
Mox ad thermās ad-
vēnērunt et in apodytērium intrāvērunt, quod iam erat plēnum puerōrum
quī ē lūdō ēgressī eō cum paedagōgīs vēnerant. Ibi vestīmenta exuēbant. 5
Marcus, vestīmentīs exūtīs, "Nunc in palaestram exeāmus," inquit. At
Eucleidēs, "Minimē!" inquit. "Pater tuus mē iussit vōs ante nōnam hōram
redūcere." Deinde alterī servō, cui nōmen erat Asellus, "Hīc manē!" inquit.
"Vestīmenta dīligenter custōdī! Hīc enim solent esse multī fūrēs quī vestīmenta surrepta in urbe vēndunt." 10
Cui Asellus respondit, "Ego semper vestīmenta dīligenter custōdiō. Nēmō
vestīmenta, mē custōde, surripere potest."
Tum puerī, vestīmentīs trāditīs, in tepidārium intrāvērunt et inde in
caldārium, ubi erat magna turba hominum. Subitō tamen exclāmāvit Sextus, "Aeger sum. Hunc calōrem patī nōn possum. Exībō et ad apodytērium 15
regrediar."
Dum ē tepidāriō exit, Asellum prope vestīmenta sedentem cōnspexit.
Dormiēbat Asellus. Eō ipsō tempore vestīmenta ā servō quōdam surripiē-
bantur. Quod ubi vīdit Sextus, "Prehende fūrem!" exclāmāvit. Simul fūr
clāmōrem Sextī audīvit, simul Asellus ē sellā exsiluit, simul Sextus ad 20
iānuam cucurrit. Fūr in palaestram cōnfūgit, nam sē in turbā cēlāre in
animō habēbat. Cum tamen inde in viam ēvādere nōn posset, in frīgidārium
fūgit.
Sextus tamen fūrem cōnspectum subsequēbātur. Fūr, Sextō vīsō, iam
valdē timēbat. In pavīmentō lāpsus in aquam frīgidam cecidit. Statim in 25
aquam dēsiluit Sextus. Fūrem ex aquā trahere cōnābātur; sed frūstrā. Cum
tamen adiūvissent adstantēs, fūr ā Sextō captus ex aquā extractus est. Quem
captum Sextus dominō trādidit.

quibus verbīs audītīs, on hearing
    these words, when they heard this
exeāmus, let us go out
fūr, fūris (m), thief

mē custōde, while I am on guard
turba, -ae (f), crowd
pavīmentum, -ī (n), tiled floor

surripiō, surripere (3), surripuī, surreptum, to steal
prehendō, prehendere (3), prehendī, prehēnsum, to seize
exsiliō, exsilīre (4), exsiluī, to leap out
cōnfugiō, cōnfugere (3), cōnfūgī, to flee for refuge
subsequor, subsequī (3), subsecūtus sum, to follow (up)
lābor, lābī (3), lāpsus sum, to slip, stumble

Iūs et fūrī dīcitur. *Justice is granted even to the thief.* (Seneca, *On Benefits* IV.28)

lapsus calami *a slip of the pen*

lapsus linguae *a slip of the tongue*

Exercise 42a

Respondē Latīnē:

1. Cūr puerī maximē gaudēbant?
2. Ubi vestīmenta exuēbant?
3. Cūr vestīmenta dīligenter custōdīrī dēbent?
4. Quid Sextus patī nōn potest?
5. Ubi sedēbat Asellus et quid faciēbat?
6. Cūr fūr in frīgidārium fūgit?
7. Quī fūrem ā Sextō captum ex aquā extrāxērunt?
8. Cui trāditus est fūr?

VERBS: Perfect Passive Participles

You have already translated sentences like the following:

Coquus vocātus ab omnibus laudātus est.
The cook, having been summoned, was praised by all.
The cook was summoned and was praised by all.

The first perfect passive participle may be translated by a main verb: "was summoned and. . . ."

Similar participial phrases appear in other cases, and the meaning of the sentence may be expressed in exactly the same way, e.g.:

Accusative:
Coquum vocātum omnēs laudāvērunt.
The cook was summoned and they all praised (him).

Dative:
Coquō vocātō omnēs grātiās ēgērunt.
The cook was summoned and they all gave thanks (to him).

There are several ways of translating sentences such as those above, e.g.:

Coquum vocātum omnēs laudāvērunt.
The cook was summoned and they all praised him.
When the cook was summoned, they all praised him.
After the cook was summoned, they all praised him.

18

Active translations are also possible, e.g.:

They all summoned the cook and praised him.
Having summoned the cook, they all praised him.
After summoning the cook, they all praised him.

VERBS: Ablative Absolute

Another arrangement is also possible:

Coquō vocātō, omnēs cēnam laudāvērunt.
The cook was summoned and *they all praised the dinner.*

Here the words **coquō vocātō** are an example of a Latin construction known as the *ablative absolute*, in which a noun (or pronoun) and a participle are in the ablative case and make up a clause which is separate from the rest of the sentence and usually set off by commas.

In addition to the translation given above, the ablative absolute **coquō vocātō** could be translated "when the cook was summoned" or "after the cook was summoned." Other clauses of this sort may best be translated with "although" or "since" or "if," depending on the context.

The participle of an ablative absolute may also be in the present tense, e.g.:

Fūre vestīmenta surripiente, Sextus in apodytērium ingreditur.
While the thief is stealing the clothes, *Sextus enters the changing room.*

The present active participle is used for an action going on at the *same time* as the action of the main verb of the sentence: the perfect passive participle is used for an action that was completed *before* the action of the main verb. Often the present participle will be translated with a past tense in English because it describes an action going on in the past at the same time as the action of the main verb in a past tense, e.g.:

Fūre vestīmenta surripiente, Sextus in apodytērium ingrediēbātur.
While the thief was stealing the clothes, *Sextus was entering the changing room.*

Since classical Latin has no present participle for the verb **esse,** ablative absolute clauses sometimes consist only of two nouns in the ablative case, e.g., **Titō prīncipe,** literally, "Titus (being) Emperor," i.e., when Titus is (was) Emperor.

Exercise 42b

Locate 5 examples of ablative absolute clauses in story 42.

19

Exercise 42c

Read aloud and translate the following sentences, giving two or three
possible translations of the participial phrases:

1. Amīcī Titum cōnspectum salūtāvērunt.
2. Titus rogātus quid in senātū agerētur, "Nihil novī," respondit.
3. Vestīmenta exūta servō trādita sunt.
4. Vestīmenta exūta Marcus servō trādidit.
5. In palaestram ingressī trigōne lūdēbant.
6. Strigilibus dēfrictī tepidārium ingressī sunt.
7. Ibi nōn diū morātī in caldārium prōcessērunt.
8. Sextus Asellum dormientem cōnspexit.
9. Clāmōribus adstantium perterritus fūr effugere cōnātus est.
10. Vestīmenta ā servō accepta puerī induērunt.

Exercise 42d

Read aloud and translate each sentence, and then identify ablative
absolute clauses. Comment on the temporal relationship between the
participle of the ablative absolute and the action of the verb in the
main clause:

1. Puerīs in lūdō clāmantibus, magister īrātus fīēbat.
2. Magistrō īrātō, puerī ē lūdō missī sunt.
3. Lūdō relictō, puerī ad thermās īvērunt.
4. Titō salūtātō, puerī in apodytērium iniērunt.
5. Vestīmentīs Asellō trāditīs, in palaestram iniērunt.
6. Lūdō cōnfectō, in tepidārium intrāvērunt.
7. Marcō in caldāriō morante, Sextus ad apodytērium regressus est.
8. Asellō dormiente, fūr vestīmenta surripuit.
9. Fūre cōnspectō, Sextus magnā vōce clāmāvit.
10. Vestīmentīs ā fūre trāditīs, puerī domum īvērunt.

> Quid rīdēs? Mūtātō nōmine dē tē fābula nārrātur. *Why do you laugh? Just
> change the name and the tale is told about you.* (Horace, *Satires* I.1.69-
> 70)

Linking quī

In story 42 you met the following:

Quibus verbīs audītīs. . . . (3)	*When they heard these words. . . .*
Cui Asellus respondit. . . . (11)	*Asellus replied to him. . . .*
Quod ubi vīdit. . . . (19)	*When he saw this. . . .*
Quem captum. . . . (27-28)	*Now that he had caught him. . . .*

20

The relative pronoun at the beginning of a sentence provides a link with a person, thing, or action in the previous sentence, e.g.:

Quibus verbīs refers to what Eucleides said in the previous sentence.
Cui refers to Eucleides who had just finished speaking.
Quod refers to the theft Sextus had just seen.
Quem refers to the thief mentioned in the previous sentence.

The Difficulty of Guarding Clothes at the Baths

Etiam quī it lavātum in balneās, cum ibi sēdulō sua vestīmenta servat, tamen surripiuntur, quippe quī quem adstantium observet falsus est. Fūr facile quī observat videt: custōs quī fūr sit nescit.

Even one who goes to the baths to bathe and watches his clothes carefully there has them stolen all the same, since he's confused as to which of the crowd to watch. The thief easily sees the one who's watching; the guard doesn't know who the thief is.

Plautus, *Rudens* 382-85 (adapted)

The Plight of a Slave from Whom His Master's Clothes Were Stolen

The following story was told by a guest at Trimalchio's dinner party:

We were just about to step into the dining room when a slave, utterly naked, landed on the floor in front of us and implored us to save him from a whipping. He was about to be flogged, he explained, for a trifling offense. He had let someone steal the steward's clothing, worthless stuff really, in the baths. Well, we pulled back our right feet, faced about and returned to the entry where we found the steward counting a stack of gold coins. We begged him to let the servant off. "Really, it's not the money I mind," he replied with enormous condescension, "so much as the idiot's carelessness. It was my dinner-suit he lost, a birthday present from one of my dependents. Expensive too, but then I've already had it washed. Well, it's a trifle. Do what you want with him." We thanked him for his gracious kindness, but when we entered the dining room up ran the same slave whom we'd just begged off. He overwhelmed us with his thanks and then, to our consternation, began to plaster us with kisses. "You'll soon see whom you've helped," he said. "The master's wine will prove the servant's gratitude."

Petronius, *Satyricon* 30-31, tr., William Arrowsmith

Versiculī: *"The Thief's Accomplice," page 117.*

21

43
Pyramus and Thisbe

In ancient Rome, the first contact the public was likely to have with a new poem or a completed section of a longer poem would be, not through reading it in a book, but through listening to it at a public reading (**recitātiō**) given by the poet in a private house or theater or recital room. Some enterprising poets even tried to gather an audience in the forum, at the Circus, or in the public baths. The large public baths often contained, in fact, libraries and reading rooms and thus catered to the minds as well as the bodies of their patrons. Martial complained of a boorish poet who pursued him wherever he went, reciting his verses: "I flee to the baths; you echo in my ear. I seek the swimming pool; you don't allow me to swim."

After the adventure with the thief, Marcus, Sextus, and Eucleides relax and enjoy listening to a recitation of one of the most famous love stories of the ancient world. The story of Pyramus and Thisbe, set in ancient Babylon and made familiar to English readers by Shakespeare's A *Midsummer Night's Dream*, was originally part of a long narrative poem called *Metamorphoses* by the Latin poet Ovid (43 B.C.–A.D. 17).

Olim Babylōne habitābat adulēscēns quīdam pulcherrimus, nōmine Pȳramus. In vīcīnā domō habitābat virgō cui nōmen erat Thisbē. Pȳramus hanc virginem in viā forte cōnspectam statim amāvit. Et Thisbē, Pȳramō vīsō, amōre capta est. Sed ēheu! Parentēs et virginis et adulēscentis, quoniam multōs iam annōs inter sē rixābantur, eōs convenīre vetuērunt. Pȳramō 5 Thisbēn nē vidēre quidem licēbat. Valdē dolēbant et adulēscēns et virgō.
Erat mūrus domuī utrīque commūnis. Parva tamen rīma, ā nūllō anteā vīsa, ab amantibus inventa est. (Quid nōn sentit amor?) Quam ad rīmam sedentēs inter sē sēcrētō colloquēbantur, alter alterī amōrem exprimēns. Sed mox, ōsculīs mūrō datīs, valedīcēbant invītī. 10
Tandem novum cōnsilium cēpērunt. Cōnstituērunt enim, parentibus īnsciīs, domō nocte exīre, in silvam convenīre, sub arbore quādam cōnsīdere. Itaque Thisbē silentiō noctis, cum vultum vēlāmine cēlāvisset, fūrtim ēgressa ad silvam festīnāvit. Quō cum advēnisset, sub illā arbore cōnsēdit. Ecce tamen vēnit leō saevus, ōre sanguine bovis aspersō. Quō cōnspectō, 15 Thisbē perterrita in spēluncam, quae prope erat, cōnfūgit. Et dum fugit, vēlāmen relīquit. Quod vēlāmen leō ōre sanguineō rapuit, sed mox dēposuit.
Haud multō post Pȳramus ex urbe ēgressus, dum ad arborem eandem progreditur, vestīgia leōnis vīdit. Subitō puellae vēlāmen sanguine aspersum cōnspexit. Timōre tremēns, "Quid accidit?" clāmāvit. "Ēheu! Ego tē occīdī, 20

22

mea Thisbē, quod tē iussī in silvam noctū sōlam venīre, nec prior vēnī.
Sine tē vīvere nōlō." Gladiō igitur strictō, sē vulnerāvit atque ad terram
cecidit moriēns.
Ecce! Metū nōndum dēpositō, Thisbē ē spēluncā timidē exit, Pȳramum
quaerit. Subitō corpus eius humī iacēns cōnspicit; multīs cum lacrimīs, 25
"Pȳrame," clāmat, "quis hoc fēcit?" Deinde, suō vēlāmine cōnspectō, iam
moritūra, "Ō mē miseram!" clāmat. "Vēlāmen meum tē perdidit. Sine tē
vīvere nōlō." Et gladiō Pȳramī ipsa sē occīdit.
Parentēs, dolōre commōtī, eōs in eōdem sepulcrō sepelīvērunt.

Babylōn, Babylōnis (f), Babylon
Pȳramus, -ī (m), Pyramus
virgō, virginis (f), maiden
Thisbē, Thisbēs (f), Thisbe
forte, by chance
rixor (1), to quarrel
uterque, utraque, utrumque, each
   (of two)
rīma, -ae (f), crack
ōsculum, -ī (n), kiss
cōnsilium, -ī (n), plan
   cōnsilium capere, to adopt a plan
īnscius, -a, -um, not knowing

vultus, -ūs (m), face
vēlāmen, vēlāminis (n), veil, shawl
saevus, -a, -um, fierce, savage
ōre sanguine aspersō, his mouth
   spattered with blood
spēlunca, -ae (f), cave
haud multō post, not much later
nec, another form of
   neque, and . . . not
prior, priōris, first (of two)
humī, on the ground
moritūra, intending to die, determined to die

sentiō, sentīre (4), sēnsī, sēnsum, to feel, notice
exprimō, exprimere (3), expressī, expressum, to express
valedīcō, valedīcere (3), valedīxī, valedictum, to say goodbye
aspergō, aspergere (3), aspersī, aspersum, to sprinkle, splash
occīdō, occīdere (3), occīdī, occīsum, to kill
vīvō, vīvere (3), vīxī, vīctum, to live
perdō, perdere (3), perdidī, perditum, to destroy

Exercise 43a

Respondē Latīnē:

1. Ubi habitābant Pȳramus et Thisbē?
2. Quandō Pȳramus Thisbēn amāvit?
3. Placuitne amor Pȳramī et Thisbēs parentibus?
4. Quid erat inter duās domūs?
5. Quid faciēbant amantēs ad rīmam mūrī sedentēs?
6. Quid faciēbat Thisbē antequam ad silvam festīnāvit?
7. Quid Thisbē in silvā vīdit?
8. Quid vīdit Pȳramus ex urbe ēgressus?
9. Cūr Pȳramus sē occīdit? Cūr Thisbē?
10. Cūr parentēs Pȳramum Thisbēnque in eōdem sepulcrō sepelīvērunt?

VERBS: *Future Active Participles*

The future active participle is usually formed by adding *-ūrus, -a, -um* to the supine stem, e.g., **portāt-: portātūrus, -a, -um.** The future active participle of some verbs ends instead in *-itūrus, -a, -um,* e.g., **moritūrus, -a, -um** (from **morior, morī, mortuus sum**):

> Thisbē . . . **iam moritūra, "Ō mē miseram!"** clāmāvit.
> *Thisbe . . . now about to die, cried, "Oh dear me!"*

The following is a tabulation of the participles in conjugations 1–4:

TENSE	ACTIVE VOICE	PASSIVE VOICE
Present	1. portāns, portantis *carrying* 2. movēns, moventis *moving* 3. mittēns, mittentis *sending* iaciēns, iacientis *throwing* 4. audiēns, audientis *hearing*	
Perfect		1. portātus, -a, -um *(having been) carried* 2. mōtus, -a, -um *(having been) moved* 3. missus, -a, -um *(having been) sent* iactus, -a, -um *(having been) thrown* 4. audītus, -a, -um *(having been) heard*
Future	1. portātūrus, -a, -um *about to carry* 2. mōtūrus, -a, -um *about to move* 3. missūrus, -a, -um *about to send* iactūrus, -a, -um *about to throw* 4. audītūrus, -a, -um *about to hear*	

Notes

1. The present and future participles are active in form and meaning.

2. The present participle of īre (*to go*) is iēns, euntis. The participles of the other irregular verbs are formed regularly, e.g., volēns, volentis. There is no present participle of esse (*to be*).

3. The future participle of īre is itūrus, -a, -um.

4. The future participle of esse is futūrus, -a, -um.

5. Other possible translations of the future participle include: "going to," "likely to," "intending to," "determined to," "on the point of . . . -ing."

6. The perfect participle is passive in form and meaning.

7. Although the participles of deponent verbs have the same endings as those of non-deponent verbs, all the meanings are active:

Present Participle	1. cōnāns, cōnantis, *trying*
	2. verēns, verentis, *fearing*
	3. loquēns, loquentis, *speaking*
	moriēns, morientis, *dying*
	4. oriēns, orientis, *rising*
Perfect Participle	1. cōnātus, -a, -um, *having tried*
	2. veritus, -a, -um, *having feared*
	3. locūtus, -a, -um, *having spoken*
	mortuus, -a, -um, *having died*
	4. ortus, -a, -um, *having risen*
Future Participle	1. cōnātūrus, -a, -um, *about to try*
	2. veritūrus, -a, -um, *about to fear*
	3. locūtūrus, -a, -um, *about to speak*
	moritūrus, -a, -um, *about to die*
	4. oritūrus, -a, -um, *about to rise*

Be sure you know all of the forms of the participles given above.

Exercise 43b

Read aloud and translate:

1. Multīs hominibus subsequentibus, fūr effugere nōn potuit.
2. Sextus fūrem effugere cōnantem subsequēbatur.
3. Puerī calōrem vix passī haud diū in caldāriō morābantur.
4. Sextus domum profectūrus ab omnibus laudātus est.
5. Thisbē moritūra ad terram cecidit.
6. Asellō custōde, vestīmenta puerōrum surrepta sunt.
7. Pȳramus ad arborem illam progrediēns vestīgia leōnis vīdit.
8. Vēlāmine relictō, Thisbē in spēluncam cōnfūgit.
9. Ad rīmam inter sē sēcrētō colloquentēs amōrem exprimēbant.
10. Pȳramus Thisbēn secūtūrus ex urbe profectus est.
11. Sōle oriente, mercātōrēs profectī sunt ad Āfricam nāvigātūrī.
12. Multa virginī pollicitus, Pȳramus eī valedīxit.

orior, orīrī (4), ortus sum, to rise
polliceor, pollicērī (2), pollicitus sum, to promise

The Fine Art of Poetry

Not all poets pursued an audience as boorishly as the versifier about whom Martial complained (see preface to this chapter). Horace (65-8 B.C.) had a far more dignified conception of his art:

Saepe stilum vertās, iterum quae digna legī sint
scrīptūrus, neque tē ut mīrētur turba labōrēs,
contentus paucīs lectōribus.

Often must you turn your pencil to erase, if you hope to write something worth a second reading, and you must not strive to catch the wonder of the crowd, but be content with the few as your readers.

Horace, *Satires* I.10.72-74

Lovers' Graffiti

I

Rōmula hīc cum Staphylō morātur.

Romula hangs around here with Staphylus.

II

Secundus cum Prīmigeniā conveniunt.

Secundus and Primigenia are going together.

III

Restitūtus multās saepe dēcēpit puellās.

Restitutus has often deceived many girls.

IV

Vibius Restitūtus hīc sōlus dormīvit et Urbānam suam dēsīderābat.

Vibius Restitutus slept here—alone—and longed for his Urbana.

V

Successus textor amat caupōniae ancillam, nōmine Hīredem, quae quidem illum nōn cūrat. Sed ille rogat illa commiserētur. Scrībit rīvālis. Valē.

Successus the weaver is in love with the hostess's maid, Iris by name, who of course doesn't care about him. But he asks that she take pity (on him). His rival is writing (this). Farewell.

VI

Quisquis amat, valeat; pereat quī nescit amāre!
Bis tantō pereat, quisquis amāre vetat!

Whoever's in love, may he succeed; whoever's not, may he perish! Twice may he perish, whoever forbids me to love!

Versiculī: *"A Difference of Opinion," page 117.*

Word Study XI

Diminutive Suffixes

When added to the base (occasionally the nominative singular) of a Latin noun or adjective, the suffixes *-ulus* (*-olus* after a vowel), *-(i)culus*, and *-ellus* (sometimes *-illus*) alter the meaning of the word by diminishing its size or importance, e.g.:

Noun or Adjective	Base (or Nom. Sing.)	Suffix	Diminutive
puer, -ī (*m*), *boy*	puer-	+ *-ulus*	= puerulus, -ī (*m*), *little boy, young slave-boy*
parvus, -a, -um, *small*	parv-	+ *-ulus*	= parvulus, -a, -um, *little, tiny*

Diminutives were sometimes used affectionately, e.g.:

filia, -ae (*f*), *daughter*	fili-	+ *-ola*	= filiola, -ae (*f*), *little daughter, darling daughter*

but they could also be disparaging, e.g.:

mulier, -is (*f*), *woman*	mulier-	+ *-cula*	= muliercula, -ae (*f*), *a little, weak, foolish woman*

Some diminutives had special meanings, e.g.:

ōs, ōris (*n*), *mouth*	ōs-	+ *-culum*	= ōsculum, -ī (*n*), *a kiss*

Adjectives formed with diminutive suffixes have endings of the 1st and 2nd declensions; diminutive nouns are in either the 1st or 2nd declension, and the gender is usually the same as that of the original noun, e.g.:

novus, -a, -um, *new*	nov-	+ *-ellus*	= novellus, -a, -um, *young, tender*
pars, partis (*f*), *part*	part-	+ *-icula*	= particula, -ae (*f*), *a little part*

English words derived from these Latin diminutives usually end in *-le*, *-ule*, *-ole*, *-cle*, *-cule*, *-el*, or *-il*, e.g., *particle, novel*.

Exercise 1

Give the meaning of the following Latin diminutives. Consult a Latin dictionary to determine what (if any) special meanings these diminutives may have had for the Romans.

1. servulus, -ī (m)
2. oppidulum, -ī (n)
3. amīcula, -ae (f)
4. lectulus, -ī (m)
5. capitulum, -ī (n)
6. cistella, -ae (f)
7. ancillula, -ae (f)
8. libellus, -ī (m)
9. lapillus, -ī (m)
10. puellula, -ae (f)

Exercise 2

Give the English word derived from each of the following Latin diminutives:

1. mūsculus, -ī (*m*), little mouse
2. circulus, -ī (*m*), a round figure
3. corpusculum, -ī (*n*), a little body
4. rīvulus, -ī (*m*), a little stream
5. minusculus, -a, -um, somewhat small
6. tabernāculum, -ī (*n*), tent

Exercise 3

Look up the Roman emperor Caligula in an encyclopedia and find out why he was known by this diminutive nickname.

Frequentative Verbs

Frequentative verbs are formed from other Latin verbs and denote repeated or intensified action. (They are also called intensive verbs.) They are usually in the first conjugation, e.g., **dictō, -āre**, *to say often, repeat* (from **dīcō, -ere**, *to say*). Often the special frequentative meaning has been lost and the frequentative verb has nearly the same meaning as the original verb, e.g., **cantō, -āre**, *to sing* (from **canō, -ere**, *to sing*). Frequentative verbs are formed from other verbs in one of two ways:

1. by adding *-ō* to the supine stem, e.g., **acceptō, -āre**, *to receive* (from **acceptum**, supine of **accipiō**)

29

2. by adding *-itō* to the base of the present infinitive (occasionally to the supine stem), e.g., **rogitō, -āre,** *to ask frequently or earnestly* (from **rogāre**), and **ēmptitō, -āre,** *to buy up* (from **ēmptum,** supine of **emō**)

Exercise 4

Give the original Latin verb to which each of the following frequentative verbs is related:

1. iactō, -āre
2. cessō, -āre
3. habitō, -āre
4. ventitō, -āre
5. haesitō, -āre
6. cursō, -āre
7. vīsitō, -āre

8. scrīptitō, -āre
9. exercitō, -āre
10. dormitō, -āre
11. clāmitō, -āre
12. ductō, -āre
13. tractō, -āre
14. agitō, -āre

Exercise 5

Look up each of the frequentative verbs in Exercise 4 in a Latin dictionary. Identify each frequentative verb whose meaning differs significantly from the meaning of the original verb.

Exercise 6

Form a frequentative verb from each of the following Latin verbs by adding *-ō* to the supine stem. Look up the frequentative verb in a Latin dictionary and compare its meaning with that of the original verb.

1. excipiō
2. reprehendō
3. olfaciō
4. expellō

5. adiuvō
6. terreō
7. gerō
8. capiō

Review X

Exercise Xa

Read aloud and translate:

Caesar Visits Britain

Gāius Iūlius Caesar, dux praeclārus Rōmānōrum, in Galliā pugnāns multa dē Britanniā cognōvit. Mercātōrēs enim ē Britanniā ad Galliam trānsgressī multa emēbant ac vēndēbant; et Britannī auxilium Gallīs Caesarī resistentibus semper mittēbant. Caesar igitur, Gallīs victīs et nāvibus parātīs, in Britanniam trānsgredī cōnstituit. Profectūrī tamen mīlitēs, magnā tempestāte coortā, nāvēs 5 cōnscendere vix poterant. Complūribus post diēbus, cum tempestāte nāvēs paene dēlētae essent, Rōmānī Britanniae appropinquantēs incolās in omnibus collibus īnstructōs cōnspexērunt. Ēgredientēs Rōmānōs Britannī, pīlīs coniectīs, dēpellere cōnātī sunt; sed, quamquam multōs Rōmānōrum vulnerāvērunt, tandem superātī sunt. 10

dux, ducis (*m*), general
pugnō (1), to fight
collis, collis (*m*), hill

īnstructus, -a, -um, drawn up, deployed
pīlum, -ī (*n*), javelin

cōnscendō, cōnscendere (3), cōnscendī, cōnscēnsum, to board (ship)
dēpellō, dēpellere (3), dēpulī, dēpulsum, to drive away

Exercise Xb

Choose the clause that could be substituted for the words quoted from the passage above and that would keep the same sense. Then translate the sentence, substituting the new clause for the original words:

1. **in Galliā pugnāns**
   a. in Galliā pugnātūrus
   b. quī in Galliā pugnābat
   c. in Galliā pugnātus
2. **ē Britanniā ad Galliam trānsgressī**
   a. quī ē Britanniā ad Galliam trānsgredientur
   b. ē Britanniā ad Galliam trānsgressūrī
   c. quī ē Britanniā ad Galliam trānsgressī sunt
3. **Gallīs victīs et nāvibus parātīs**
   a. cum Gallī victī essent et nāvēs essent parātae
   b. Gallōs victūrus et nāvēs parātūrus
   c. Gallōs vincēns et nāvēs parāns

31

4. **profectūrī tamen mīlitēs**
   a. profectīs tamen mīlitibus
   b. mīlitēs tamen quī proficīscī in animō habēbant
   c. mīlitēs tamen quī profectī essent

5. **cum tempestāte nāvēs paene dēlētae essent**
   a. tempestāte nāvēs paene dēlente
   b. quod tempestāte nāvēs paene dēlētae sunt
   c. nāvibus tempestāte paene dēlētīs

6. **quamquam multōs Rōmānōrum vulnerāvērunt**
   a. multīs Rōmānīs vulnerātīs
   b. multōs Rōmānōrum vulnerātūrī
   c. multī Rōmānōrum vulnerātī

Exercise Xc

Read the following passage and answer the questions below in English:

The Sabine Women

Rōmulus, cum urbem Rōmam condidisset, quod in urbe erant paucī modo cīvēs, plūrimōs praedōnēs hominēsque scelestōs sine discrīmine ē vīcīnīs populīs in urbem accēpit. Sed pēnūria erat mulierum. Virī igitur, īrātī quod nūllās uxōrēs habēbant, cum ad Rōmulum adiissent, "Nisi nōbīs," inquiunt, "uxōrēs invēneris, urbem relinquēmus." Tum ē cōnsiliō senātōrum Rōmulus 5 nūntiōs circā vīcīnōs populōs mīsit, quī societātem cōnūbiumque petēbant. Nusquam tamen cōmiter acceptī sunt.

Deinde Rōmulus, cōnsiliō callidō captō, in magnō agrō quī haud longē ab urbe aberat lūdōs Neptūnō magnificōs parāvit. Sabīnōrum omnis multitūdō invītāta cum līberīs ac uxōribus vēnit. Quī cum mūrōs et multās domōs urbis 10 vīdissent, mīrātī sunt quod urbs Rōma tam brevī tempore crēverat.

Cum spectāculī tempus vēnisset dēditaeque eō mentēs cum oculīs essent, subitō Rōmānī, signō datō, in multitūdinem adstantium incurrērunt. Virginēs abripuērunt. Ubīque erat clāmor et tumultus. Fīliae Sabīnōrum raptae in urbem tractae sunt lacrimantēs. Parentēs virginum perterritī et trīstissimī fūgē- 15 runt. Iam tandem Rōmānī uxōrēs habēbant.

pēnūria, -ae (f), shortage
ē cōnsiliō, following the advice
circā (+ acc.), around
societātem cōnūbiumque, alliance
   and right to intermarry
callidus, -a, -um, cunning, ingenious

Sabīnī, -ōrum (m pl), the Sabines,
   a people to the north-east of
   Rome
dēditae eō, concentrated on it
mēns, mentis (f), mind
ubīque, everywhere

mīror, mīrārī (1), mīrātus sum, to be amazed, marvel (at)
crēscō, crēscere (3), crēvī, crētum, to grow, develop

1. When and why did Romulus receive thieves and wicked men from neighboring peoples into his city?
2. Why were these men angry?
3. What did they threaten to do?
4. Whose advice did Romulus take?
5. What did his messengers seek?
6. Who formed an ingenious plan?
7. Whom did Romulus invite to the games in honor of Neptune?
8. What amazed the Sabines? When?
9. At what moment did the Romans rush upon the Sabines?
10. What were the feelings of the Sabine girls and of their parents?

Exercise Xd

In the passage in Exercise Xc, locate the following in sequence:

1. All verbs in the pluperfect active subjunctive.
2. All ablative absolutes.
3. Linking quī.

44
A Rainy Day

Many of the games that children play today were also played by Roman children. They built toy houses and rode on long sticks; they had spinning tops, hoops that they bowled along with a stick, and dolls (**pūpae**); they tossed coins, calling out "heads or ships" (**capita aut nāvia**); and they played at being soldiers or judges or consuls. They also used to harness mice to toy carts.

Nuts were used in several children's games. One nut was balanced on three others, and children competed at knocking them down with a fruit stone. The winner got all the nuts. They also competed at throwing nuts into a narrow-necked vase that had been placed some distance away from them. A very popular game was to ask your partner to guess whether the number of nuts or pebbles or other similar objects that you had in your hand was odd or even (**pār impār**). In another popular game two players each showed (or "flashed") a number of fingers on their right hands (**digitīs micāre**) and simultaneously called out how many fingers altogether they believed had been shown. The round was won by the player who first guessed correctly five times. This game is still played in Italy under the name of *morra*.

Both adults and children played a game that resembled checkers or chess (**lūdus latrunculōrum**, "game of bandits"), in which they moved two sets of pieces on a checkered board. They also played a game of chance with knucklebones or dice (**tālī**). Older children and young men took exercise on the Campus Martius—wrestling, riding, and driving chariots—followed possibly by a swim across the Tiber.

As we rejoin our story, Marcus and Sextus are spending a rainy day at home.

"Ēheu!" mussāvit Marcus. "Cūr 'ēheu'?" rogāvit Sextus.

"Semper pluit!" respondit Marcus. "Ego in animō habēbam ad Campum Martium hodiē dēscendere et ad palaestram īre, sed pater nōs domī manēre iussit. Putō patrem esse crūdēlem."

Eō ipsō tempore Eucleidēs ingressus puerōs rogāvit cūr tam trīstēs essent. 5

"In palaestram īre cupiēbāmus," inquit Marcus, "sed pater hoc vetuit."

Cui Eucleidēs, "Bonō animō este!" inquit. "Ego vōs docēbō latrunculīs lūdere. Putō hunc lūdum esse optimum."

Duās ferē hōrās ita lūdēbant. Postrēmō Sextus exclāmāvit, "Hic lūdus mē nōn iam dēlectat. Ego putō hunc lūdum esse pessimum. Age, Marce! 10 Nōnne vīs pār impār lūdere vel digitīs micāre?"

Statim clāmāre coepērunt ambō. Simul Marcus, "Quīnque!," simul Sextus, "Novem!" deinde Marcus, "Octō!," Sextus, "Sex!"
"Tacēte, puerī!" interpellāvit Eucleidēs. "Nōlīte clāmōribus vestrīs vexāre mātrem et Cornēliam! Putō vōs esse molestissimōs hodiē." At puerī eī nōn 15 pārēbant. Itaque Cornēlia, clāmōribus audītīs, in ātrium ingressa rogāvit quid facerent.
"Nōlī nōs vexāre!" inquit Sextus. "Abī! Sed cūr pūpam in manibus habēs? Num pūpā lūdis?"
"Stultus es, Sexte! Pūpa nōn est mea. Num crēdis mē pūpā lūdere? Hanc 20 pūpam, quam ego ipsa fēcī, fīliae Dāvī dōnō dabō. Hodiē est diēs nātālis eius."
Subitō Sextus, pūpā abreptā, in peristȳlium aufūgit. Quō vīsō, Eucleidēs Sextō clāmāvit. "Nōlī pūpam laedere! Statim eam refer!"
Eō ipsō tempore ingressus est Cornēlius. Cum audīvisset quid Sextus 25 fēcisset, "Sexte!" clāmāvit. "Venī hūc!" Puer, iam timidus, in ātrium regressus pūpam Cornēliae reddidit. Tum Cornēlius Sextum sēcum ex ātriō ēdūxit.
Quō factō, Marcus rogāvit, "Quid pater faciet? Quid Sextō fiet?"
Cui Cornēlia, "Putō," inquit, "patrem in animō habēre Sextum verberāre." 30

putō (1), to think, consider
Bonō animō es (este)! Cheer up!
lūdus, -ī (m), game
ferē, almost, approximately
postrēmō, finally
ambō, ambae, ambō, both
pūpa, -ae (f), doll

Num . . . ? Surely . . . not . . . ?
dōnō dare, to give as a gift
diēs nātālis, birthday
peristȳlium, -ī (n), peristyle, courtyard surrounded with a colonnade
Quid Sextō fiet? What will happen
  to Sextus?

laedō, laedere (3), laesī, laesum, to harm

Exercise 44a

Using story 44 as a guide, give the Latin for:

1. Marcus intended to go to the exercise ground today.
2. Eucleides will teach the boys to play "bandits."
3. He thinks that this is a very good game.
4. Both boys began to shout and annoy their mother and Cornelia.
5. Eucleides thinks that the boys are very annoying today.
6. The boys do not obey the slave.
7. Sextus believes that Cornelia is playing with a doll.
8. Cornelia is going to give the doll as a gift to the daughter of Davus.
9. Sextus snatches the doll and flees into the courtyard.
10. Cornelia believes that her father intends to beat Sextus.

35

Accusative and Infinitive (Indirect Statement) I

The following sentences occurred in the story:

Putō **hunc lūdum esse** optimum.
I think that this game is a very good one.

Putō **vōs esse** molestissimōs.
I think that you are very annoying.

Num crēdis **mē pūpā lūdere?**
Surely you do not believe that I am playing with a doll?

In such sentences, you are being given two pieces of information:

(1) I think   (2) what I think
   Putō   hunc lūdum esse optimum.
                   (that) this game is a very good one.

You will see that, in the second part, the Latin subject is expressed in the *accusative* case and the verb is in the *infinitive*, where English says "that this game" and "is." Similarly:

Sciō	vōs esse molestissimōs.
I know *that*	*you are very troublesome.*
Vidēmus	Dāvum in agrīs labōrāre.
We see *that*	*Davus is working in the fields.*
Audiō	eum domī morārī.
I hear *that*	*he is staying at home.*

Other verbs which may be followed by the *accusative and infinitive* construction include **dīcō** (I say), **spērō** (I hope), and **sentiō** (I feel).

Sextus sentit **sē** aegrum **esse.**
Sextus feels that he is ill.

In translating this Latin construction, the next English word after verbs such as "I think," "I know," "I see," "I hear," and "I feel" will most often be "that."

This accusative and infinitive construction in which something is being reported indirectly is known as *indirect statement*.

36

Exercise 44b

Read aloud and translate:

1. Eucleidēs dīcit lūdum latrunculōrum esse optimum.
2. Sciō Cornēlium esse senātōrem Rōmānum.
3. Nōs omnēs scīmus Cornēliam esse puellam Rōmānam.
4. Putō Sextum puerum temerārium esse.
5. Audiō Cornēlium ad Cūriam festīnāre.
6. Scit ancillās cēnam parāre.
7. Videō haud longam esse viam.
8. Audiō caupōnem esse amīcum Eucleidis.
9. Putāmus in agrīs labōrāre servōs.
10. Crēdō Aurēliam ad urbem proficīscī.
11. Dīcunt Marcum dormīre.
12. Scīmus semper ēsurīre puerōs.
13. Audiō Titum mappam nōn habēre.
14. Cornēlia putat pūpam esse pulcherrimam.

Exercise 44c

Select, read aloud, and translate:

1. Aliī putant (Sextus/Sextum) esse bonum, aliī putant eum (est/erat/esse) molestum.
2. Dāvus quidem scit omnēs (puerōs/puerum/puerī) saepe esse (molestum/molestī/molestōs).
3. At Aurēlia putat Marcum et Sextum semper bonōs (sunt/esse/erant).
4. Sextus Marcō dīcit Dāvum (esse/est/sum) īrācundum.
5. Semper respondet Marcus (Dāvī/Dāvō/Dāvum) nōn (esse/est) īrācundum.
6. Dīcit Dāvum in agrīs dīligenter (labōrāre/labōrāvit/labōrat).
7. Sextus respondet Dāvum sub arbore cotīdiē post merīdiem (dormīs/dormiēbat/dormīre).
8. Cornēlia putat (puerī/puerīs/puerōs) haud dīligenter (labōrāvērunt/labōrant/labōrāre).
9. Dīcit Cornēlia Marcum et (Sextī/Sextum/Sextus) saepe in lectō diū (iacēre/iacent/iacēmus).
10. Flāvia, amīca Cornēliae, putat (Cornēlia/Cornēliam/Cornēliae) puellam pulcherrimam (esse/sunt/est).

37

Games Played by Children and Adults

A poet describes games boys play with nuts (**nucēs**):

Hās puer aut certō rēctās dīlāminat ictū
    aut prōnās digitō bisve semelve petit.
These (nuts), as they stand upright, a boy splits with certain aim,
    or, as they lie on their side, strikes with his finger once or twice.

Quattuor in nucibus, nōn amplius, ālea tōta est,
    cum sibi suppositīs additur ūna tribus.
In four nuts, and no more, is all his hazard,
    when one is added to the three beneath it.

Per tabulae clīvum lābī iubet alter et optat
    tangat ut ē multīs quaelibet ūna suam.
Another has them roll down a sloping board, and prays
    that one out of many, whichever it may be, may touch his own.

Est etiam, pār sit numerus quī dīcat an impār,
    ut dīvīnātās auferat augur opēs.
Then there is (a boy) who guesses whether the number be odd or even,
    that the augur may bear away the wealth he has divined.

Fit quoque dē crētā, quālem caeleste figūram
    sīdus et in Graecīs littera quarta gerit.
Then too there is drawn in chalk a shape, such as a heavenly
    constellation or the fourth Greek letter bears.

Haec ubi distincta est gradibus, quae cōnstitit intus
    quot tetigit virgās, tot capit ipsa nucēs.
When this has been marked with stages, the nut that stops within it
    gains itself as many nuts as it has touched lines.

Women playing knucklebones.

Vās quoque saepe cavum spatiō distante locātur,
    in quod missa levī nux cadat ūna manū.

Often too a hollow vessel is placed at a distance,
    into which a nut flung by a skillful hand may fall.

Ovid, *Nux* 73-86

The next two passages refer to playing **pār impār** by flashing the fingers
(**micāre**):

When they praise a man's honesty, they say, "He is a man with whom you
can safely play at odd and even in the dark."

Cicero, *De officiis* III.77

"Suppose there were two men to be saved from a sinking ship—both of
them wise men—and only one small plank. Should both seize it to save
themselves? Or should one give way to the other?"

"Why, of course one should give way to the other, but that other must
be the one whose life is more valuable, either for his own sake or for that
of his country."

"But what if these considerations are of equal weight in both?"

"Then there will be no contest, but one will give place to the other, as
if the point were decided by lot or at a game of odd and even."

Cicero, *De officiis* III.90

Gambling with Dice (tālī—compare Chapter 32)

From a personal letter of the Emperor Augustus:

I dined, dear Tiberius, with the same company; we had besides as guests
Vinicius and the elder Silius. We gambled like old men during the meal
both yesterday and today. When the dice were thrown, whoever turned up
the "dog" or the six put a denarius in the pool for each one of the dice
and the whole was taken by anyone who threw the "Venus."

From a personal letter of the Emperor Augustus to his daughter:

I send you two hundred and fifty denarii, the sum that I gave each of my
guests, in case they wished to play at dice or at odd and even during the
dinner.

Suetonius, *Augustus* LXXI.2, 4

The Last Move in a Game of Chess (lūdus latrun-culōrum)

Julius Canus, after a long dispute with the Emperor Caligula, was ordered
by the capricious emperor to be executed. Seneca the moralist praises the
bravery of Canus under sentence of death:

39

Will you believe that Canus spent the ten intervening days before his execution in no anxiety of any sort? What the man said, what he did, how tranquil he was, passes all credence. He was playing chess when the centurion who was dragging off a whole company of victims to death ordered that he also be summoned. Having been called, he counted the pawns and said to his partner: "See that after my death you do not claim falsely that you won." Then nodding to the centurion, he said, "You will bear witness that I am one pawn ahead."

Seneca, *De tranquillitate* XIV.6-7

Quid est tam incertum quam tālōrum iactus? *What is so uncertain as a cast of dice?* (Cicero, *De divinatione* II.121)

nucēs relinquere *to leave childhood behind* (Persius, *Satires* I.10)

The Irregular Verb *fīō, fierī, factus sum*

This irregular verb, meaning "to become," "to be made," or "to happen," serves as the passive of **faciō**. Some of its forms were introduced in Exercise 32e. Its forms in the present, imperfect, and future tenses are as follows:

		Present	*Imperfect*	*Future*
S	1	fīō	fiēbam	fīam
	2	fīs	fiēbās	fīēs
	3	fit	fiēbat	fīet
P	1	fīmus	fiēbāmus	fīēmus
	2	fītis	fiēbātis	fīētis
	3	fiunt	fiēbant	fīent

Learn the above forms thoroughly.

Exercise 44d

Read aloud and translate:

1. Titus vīnum bibit et paulātim ēbrius fit.
2. Sī Titus plūs vīnī bibet, magis ēbrius fiet.
3. Aurēlia Titum in diēs molestiōrem fierī putat.
4. Quid Titō fiet sī etiam plūs vīnī nunc bibet?
5. Aliquid malī certē eī fiet.

Versiculī: *"Sextus Reproved," page 118.*

40

Circus and Arena

The Romans did not have regular sporting events as we have at weekends, or organized entertainment available every day as we have in the theater or cinema. Instead, to celebrate religious festivals, commemorate great national victories, or honor the emperor, there were public holidays. These lasted a varying number of days, during which entertainments were presented in the circus and the arena. The number of these festivals increased as time went on until, by the reign of Claudius, 159 days of the year were holidays.

Admission to the shows was free, and all the emperors made sure there was plenty of entertainment. According to Fronto:

> Trajan sensibly always paid attention to the idols of the theater, the circus, or the arena because he knew that the entertainment of the people was very important to the government; doling out corn or money might keep individuals quiet, but shows were necessary to keep the mob happy.
>
> Fronto, *Preamble to History* 17

Juvenal, too, refers to the demand of the Roman mob for **pānem et circēnsēs**—the bread-dole and games in the Circus.

The cost of the public games was met by the state. Often, magistrates added to the grant from their own pockets in order to increase their popularity and the chance of success in their careers. To do this they even ran into debt:

> Julius Caesar spent money so recklessly that many thought he was paying a high price to create a short-lived sensation, but really he was buying very cheaply the most powerful position in the world. Before entering politics he was thirteen hundred talents in debt. As aedile he staged games with 320 pairs of gladiators fighting in single combat. In this and his other extravagance in presenting theatrical performances, processions, and public banquets, he completely outdid all previous efforts to obtain publicity in this way.
>
> Plutarch, *Caesar* 5

41

45
Looking Forward to the Games

Postrīdiē, dum Gāius Cornēlius in tablīnō scrībit, subitō intrāvit Titus, frāter eius.

"Salvē, Gāī!" clāmāvit Titus. "Quid agis?"

"Bene!" respondit Cornēlius. "Sed semper sum, ut vidēs, negōtiōsus."

Cui Titus, "Prō certō habeō tē crās nōn labōrātūrum esse. Omnēs enim 5 cīvēs Rōmānī ad mūnera itūrī sunt. Spērō tē quoque ad mūnera itūrum esse."

At Cornēlius, "Mūnera?" inquit. "Quid dīcis, mī Tite?"

"Prō dī immortālēs!" exclāmāvit Titus. "Crās Caesar amphitheātrum aperiet novum. Tū tamen rogās quid dīcam?" 10

Cornēlius autem cum rīsū, "Nōnne sentīs mē per iocum hoc dīxisse? Certē hic diēs maximē omnium memorābilis erit. Cōnstat Iūdaeōs dīligenter labōrāvisse et amphitheātrum summā celeritāte cōnfēcisse. Nōs templum illōrum dēlēvimus, illī amphitheātrum aedificāvērunt nostrum."

Cui Titus, "Mehercule! Tōtum populum continēbit hoc amphitheātrum. 15 Crās māne viae erunt plēnae hominum quī ab omnibus partibus ad spectāculum congredientur."

"Ita!" inquit Cornēlius. "Putō tamen Aurēliam eō nōn itūram esse. Scīs enim Aurēliam neque mūnera neque sanguinem amāre. Aurēlia domī manēre māvult. Marcum tamen mēcum sum ductūrus. Iam adulēscēns est et 20 mox togam virīlem sūmet. Sextus autem, quod adhūc puer est, domī manēbit; nam, ut docet Seneca, 'Quō maior populus, eō plūs perīculī.' Quotā hōrā tū ad amphitheātrum crās māne es itūrus?"

"Prīmā lūce," respondit Titus, "nam mātūrē advenīre in animō habeō. Quandō tū et Marcus eō perveniētis?" 25

"Haud mātūrē," inquit Cornēlius, "sed prō certō habeō nōs tē in amphitheātrō vīsūrōs esse. Nunc haec epistula est cōnficienda. Valē!"

"Valē!" inquit Titus. "Nōs abitūrī tē salūtāmus!"

negōtiōsus, -a, -um, busy	**māvult,** (she) prefers
prō certō habeō, I am sure	**quō maior . . . , eō plūs . . . ,** the
mūnera, mūnerum (*n pl*), games	greater . . . , the more . . .
spērō (1), to hope	**mātūrē,** early
cōnstat, it is agreed	**epistula est cōnficienda,** the letter
Iūdaeī, Iūdaeōrum (*m pl*), Jews	must be finished
mālō, mālle, māluī, to prefer	

Exercise 45a

Respondē Latīnē:

1. Quandō intrāvit Titus tablīnum Gāiī?
2. Quālis vir est Cornēlius?
3. Quō cīvēs Rōmānī crās ībunt?
4. Quid Caesar crās faciet?
5. Quālis diēs erit crās?
6. Quid Iūdaeī aedificāvērunt?
7. Quid Rōmānī dēlēvērunt?
8. Unde hominēs ad spectāculum congredientur?
9. Cūr Aurēlia domī manēre māvult?
10. Quis cum Cornēliō ad mūnera ībit?
11. Cūr Sextus domī manēbit?
12. Quotā hōrā Titus ad amphitheātrum crās ībit?
13. Quem putat Cornēlius sē in amphitheātrō crās vīsūrum esse?
14. Quid Cornēlius nunc cōnficere vult?

Accusative and Infinitive (Indirect Statement) II

The future infinitive and the perfect infinitive are also used in indirect statements. Look at the following examples:

Putō Aurēliam eō nōn **itūram esse.**
*I think that Aurelia **will** not go there.*

Prō certō habeō nōs tē **vīsūrōs esse.**
*I am sure that we **will see** you.*

The phrases **itūram esse** and **vīsūrōs esse** are *future active infinitives.* You will recognize this form as **esse** with the future participle, which appears in the accusative case agreeing with the subject of the infinitive clause in gender, case, and number. (For the future participle, see Chapter 43.)

Cōnstat Iūdaeōs dīligenter **labōrāvisse** et amphitheātrum summā celeritāte **cōnfēcisse.**
*It is agreed that the Jews **have worked** hard and **finished** the amphitheater very quickly.*

The *perfect active infinitive* (**labōrāvisse** and **cōnfēcisse**) can be recognized by the ending -**isse**, which is added to the perfect stem. (See Chapter 40.)

When **sē** is used in the accusative and infinitive construction in indirect statements, it is translated "he," "she," or "they," and refers to the subject of the verb of *saying, thinking,* or *hearing,* e.g.:

Titus dīxit sē ad amphitheātrum itūrum esse.
*Titus said that **he** would go to the amphitheater.*

43

The use of **sē** in this sentence shows that "he" refers to Titus. If the "he" had referred to someone else, **eum** would have been used instead of **sē**.

Puellae puerīs dīxērunt sē eōs adiūtūrās esse.
The girls told the boys that they would help them.

In this sentence, **sē** must refer to **puellae**, and the future infinitive **adiūtūrās esse** is feminine accusative plural agreeing with **sē**, while **eōs** refers to **puerīs**.

Adulēscēns spērat sē diū vīctūrum esse; senex potest dīcere sē diū vīxisse.
A young man hopes that he will live a long time; an old man is able to say that he has lived a long time. (adapted from Cicero, *On Old Age* XIX.68)

Exercise 45b

Read aloud and translate:

1. Putāmus servōs dīligenter labōrātūrōs esse.
2. Putāsne patruum tuum ad amphitheātrum pervēnisse?
3. Cōnstat illum diem memorābilem fuisse.
4. Scīs Cornēliam domī mānsūram esse.
5. Cornēlius audit Titum domum nōn vēnisse.
6. Cornēlius putat Aurēliam in peristȳliō ambulātūram esse.
7. Scīmus Sextum ad patrem suum epistulam scrīpsisse.
8. Audīmus Caesarem amphitheātrum novum aperuisse.
9. Scīmus omnēs cīvēs Rōmānōs ad mūnera itūrōs esse.
10. Spērat Aurēlia Cornēlium domum festīnātūrum esse.

Exercise 45c

Select, read aloud, and translate:

1. Prō certō habeō puerum (ventūrus/ventūrum/ventūrōs) esse.
2. Putāmus mīlitēs tribus diēbus (adventūrōs/adventūrās/adventūram) esse.
3. Spērō tē, Cornēlia, mox (reditūrus/reditūram/reditūrum) esse.
4. Scīmus (eam/eōs/eum) mox ingressūram esse.
5. Putat (omnēs/nēminem/paucōs) discessūrum esse.
6. Spērāsne (eōs/eum/eam) secūtūrōs esse?
7. Scīsne puellās crās (abitūrās esse/abīre/abiisse)?
8. Audīvī Iūdaeōs paucīs diēbus amphitheātrum (cōnficere/cōnfectūrum esse/cōnfectūrōs esse).
9. Respondent servī sē heri quam celerrimē (currere/cucurrisse/cursūrōs esse).
10. Eucleidēs dīcit sē epistulam crās (cōnficere/cōnfēcisse/cōnfectūrum esse).

44

The Colosseum

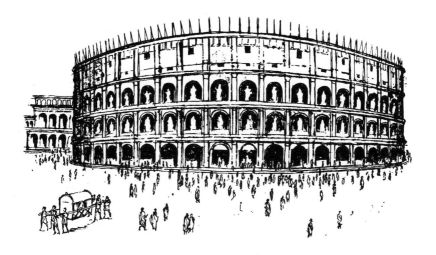

When the family of Cornelius returned to Rome, the great building of the Colosseum was nearing completion. Until this time, Rome's amphitheaters had usually been temporary wooden structures and these caused some frightful disasters, as at Fidenae near Rome in A.D. 27, when a wooden amphitheater collapsed, killing or maiming 50,000 people. Wooden structures continued to be built even after the completion of the magnificent architectural monument known to its contemporaries as the **Amphitheātrum Flāvium** but familiar to us as the Colosseum, so named from the nearly colossal statue of Nero, converted by Vespasian into a statue of the sun-god.

Begun by Vespasian, the Colosseum was dedicated in June, A.D. 80, by his son Titus, who had used Jewish prisoners to speed up its construction. The massive elliptical building rose in four tiers and measured overall 620 × 512 feet or 189 × 156 meters. With seating space estimated at 45,000, it could be covered over by a massive awning in excessive heat or rain—though Gaius Caligula is said to have taken delight in opening such awnings in times of extreme heat and forbidding anyone to leave! It took 1,000 sailors of the Imperial fleet to raise this awning.

Admission was free and open to men, women, and children, slave or free, so long as places were available. Women were confined to the topmost area and their view must certainly have been restricted.

45

The floor of the Colosseum was of timber, strewn with sand, and would contain numerous trapdoors. Under the arena, and extending beyond it, was a vast complex of subterranean cells and passages which now lie open and exposed to view. Remains can be seen of lifts and machinery (worked by counterweights) used to raise, at various points in the arena, caged animals, scenery, and other apparatus needed for wild beast hunts.

On the occasion of the dedication of the Colosseum, Emperor Titus held a festival for 100 days and during the celebrations staged a very lavish gladiatorial show.

The interior of the Colosseum as it is today. (Peter Clayton)

The Irregular Verb mālō, mālle, māluī

The verb mālō is a compound of the adverb magis and the irregular verb volō, and it means "to wish more," "to wish rather," or "to prefer." It has no imperative. Its forms in the present, imperfect, and future tenses are as follows:

		Present	Imperfect	Future
S	1	mālō	mālēbam	mālam
	2	māvīs	mālēbās	mālēs
	3	māvult	mālēbat	mālet
P	1	mālumus	mālēbāmus	mālēmus
	2	māvultis	mālēbātis	mālētis
	3	mālunt	mālēbant	mālent

Learn the above forms thoroughly.

Note carefully which forms contain the letter *l* and which the letter *v* in the present tense. The imperfect and future are regular.

Review the forms of volō and nōlō in the Forms section at the end of this book before doing the following exercise.

Exercise 45d

For each form of the verb volō, substitute the corresponding form of the verb nōlō, read aloud, and translate. Then substitute the corresponding forms of mālō, read aloud, and translate.

1. Titus trigōne lūdere volēbat.
2. Puerī ad thermās īre volunt.
3. "In silvam convenīre volumus," inquiunt Pȳramus et Thisbē.
4. "Ad amphitheātrum crās īre volam," inquit Marcus.
5. Titus prīmā lūce ad amphitheātrum īre vult.
6. Sciō puerōs prīmā lūce surgere velle.
7. Cūr pār impār lūdere vīs, Marce?
8. "Vultisne latrunculīs lūdere, puerī?" inquit Eucleidēs.
9. "Dormīre volō," inquit Sextus.
10. Cornēliī ad vīllam rūsticam mox redīre volent.
11. Sciō Aurēliam herī domī manēre voluisse.

Dīmidium dōnāre Linō quam crēdere tōtum
   quī māvult, māvult perdere dīmidium.
*Whoever prefers to give Linus half rather than trust him
   with the whole, prefers to lose the half.* Martial, *Epigrams* I.75

Martial, De spectaculis

Born in Bilbilis, Spain, about A.D. 40, Martial went to Rome in A.D. 64, the year of the Great Fire, when Nero was Emperor. His fame as a keen observer of life in the City and as a composer of biting, satirical epigrams rests on poems he published in great numbers between A.D. 86 and 98. In A.D. 80, the year in which the Flavian Amphitheater was dedicated, Martial wrote a group of epigrams which he published under the title *De spectaculis*, in which he describes many of the memorable combats that took place in the arena that year. The first three poems in the collection are given below. In the first, Martial tries to assess the importance of the Amphitheater as an architectural monument. In the second he describes the joy of the Roman people in the building program of Vespasian and Titus that replaced the hated **Domus Aurea** of Nero with structures of more use to the people. In the third he pictures the influx of people from all over the Roman world who came to the dedication ceremonies.

(i)

Do not let barbarian Memphis tell of the wonder of her Pyramids, nor Assyrian toil vaunt its Babylon; let not the soft Ionians be praised for Trivia's temple; let the altar built of many horns keep its Delos hidden; let not Carians exalt to the skies with excessive praise the Mausoleum poised on empty air. The results of all these labors of man yield to Caesar's Amphitheater. One work in place of all shall Fame rehearse.

(ii)

Here where, rayed with stars, the Colossus has a close view of heaven, and in the middle of the way tall scaffolds rise, hatefully gleamed the palace of a savage king, and only a single House then stood in all the City. Here, where the far-seen Amphitheater lifts its mass august, was Nero's lake. Here where we admire the warm baths, a gift swiftly built, a proud domain had robbed the poor of their dwellings. Where the Claudian Colonnade extends its outspread shade, the Palace ended in its farthest part. Now Rome is restored to itself, and under your rule, Caesar, what had been the delight of a tyrant is now the delight of the people.

(iii)

What nation is so far distant, what people so barbarous, Caesar, that a spectator has not come from one of them to your city? A farmer of Rhodope has come from Orphic Haemus; a Sarmatian fed on draughts of horses' blood has come; and he who drinks at its source the stream of first-found Nile, and he whose shore the wave of farthest Tethys beats; the Arab has hurried here, Sabaeans have hurried, and Cilicians have here been drenched in their own saffron dew. With hair twined in a knot Sygambrians have come, and Aethiopians with their locks twined in other ways. The languages of the peoples are varied, yet they are one when you are acclaimed your country's true father.

48

46
A Day at
the Colosseum

A day at the Colosseum was a great occasion. Tickets (**tesserae**), shown to the gate-keepers (**appāritōrēs**), were numbered according to the seating areas in the Amphitheater. Seventy-six main entrances and numerous marble plaques illustrating the seating areas enabled the spectators to move swiftly and efficiently through a network of passages, stairs, and ramps to their correct place. The officiating magistrate, usually the Emperor in Rome, would go to the imperial seat of honor (**pulvīnar**); and then the show could begin. The gladiators would parade and stop before the **pulvīnar**; they would greet the emperor with the words: "Hail, Caesar! Those who are about to die give you greetings." (**Avē, Caesar! Moritūrī tē salūtant.**) Next the band (**cornicinēs** and **tubicinēs**) would strike up. Then came the games. Pairs (**paria**) of gladiators would fight, urged on by the trainers (**lanistae**). The people joined in with roars of "Thrash him!" (**Verberā!**), "Murder him!" (**Iugulā!**), "He's hit!" (**Hoc habet!**), "Let him go!" (**Mitte!**). The savagery reached a peak with the midday fighters (**merīdiānī**), usually condemned criminals.

Marcus and his father go to the amphitheater early in the morning as planned.

Prope amphitheātrum omnēs viae erant plēnae hominum quī ad spectāculum veniēbant. Undique clāmor ac strepitus; undique cīvēs, fēminae, servī. Multī tōtam noctem extrā amphitheātrī portās morātī erant. Nunc adfuit hōra spectāculī.

Cornēlius, cum tesserās appāritōribus ostendisset, ad locum magistrātibus 5 reservātum cum Marcō ā servō ductus est. Marcus tot et tam variōs hominēs numquam vīderat. Dum attonitus circumspicit, subitō vīdit Titum iam cōnsēdisse. Patruum rogāre cupiēbat quandō pervēnisset, nam sciēbat Titum sērō ē lectō surgere solēre. Sed, quod pater aderat, Marcus nihil dīxit. Quam ingēns erat amphitheātrum! Quanta erat spectātōrum turba! Marcus coni- 10 ciēbat quot spectātōrēs amphitheātrō continērī possent cum subitō fuit silentium. Omnēs ad pulvīnar oculōs convertērunt.

"Ecce!" clāmāvit Titus. "Iam intrat Caesar, amor ac dēliciae generis hūmānī!"

49

Tum, clāmōre sublātō, spectātōrēs prīncipem ūnā vōce salūtāvērunt. 15
Stupuit Marcus, admīrātiōne captus. Iam gladiātōrēs cūnctī contrā pulvīnar
cōnstiterant. "Avē, Caesar!" clāmāvērunt. "Moritūrī tē salūtant." Exiērunt
gladiātōrēs. Mox tubicinēs et cornicinēs. Postrēmō gladiātōrum paria in
arēnam intrāvērunt.
Nunc undique erat clāmor, tumultus, furor. Lanistae hūc illūc concur- 20
santēs, "Verberā!" "Iugulā!" clāmābant; turba, "Hoc habet!" aut, "Mitte!"
aut, "Iugulā!" Marcus nihil tāle prius vīderat. Complūrēs hōrās ācriter
pugnābātur; haud minus ferōciter ā spectātōribus clāmābātur.
Subitō Cornēlius, "Nunc," inquit, "domum nōbīs redeundum est. Mox
enim pugnābunt merīdiānī, quōs aliās tū, Marce, vidēbis."   25
"Nōnne tū quoque discēdere vīs, patrue?" clāmāvit Marcus.
Cui respondit Titus sē discēdere nōlle; sē nōndum satis vīdisse; merīdiānōs
mox in arēnam ventūrōs esse. Brevī tempore Marcus cum Cornēliō in lectīcā
per urbem portābātur et sēcum cōgitābat, "Quid ego prīmum Sextō nārrābō?"

tot, so many	furor, furōris (m), frenzy
coniciēbat, was trying to guess	prius, previously
amor ac dēliciae generis hūmānī,	ācriter, fiercely
the darling and delight of man-	pugnābātur, the fighting went on
kind	nōbīs redeundum est, we must re-
admīrātiōne captus, in utter	turn
amazement	aliās, at another time
contrā (+ acc.), opposite, in front	
of, facing	

ostendō, ostendere (3), ostendī, ostentum, to show, point out
convertō, convertere (3), convertī, conversum, to turn (around)
tollō, tollere (3), sustulī, sublātum, to lift, raise
cōnsistō, cōnsistere (3), cōnstitī, to halt, stop, stand

Quot hominēs, tot sententiae. *Everyone has his own opinion.* (Terence,
Phormio 454)

Exercise 46a

Read aloud and translate:

1. Titus respondet sē domum redīre nōlle.
2. Nōs omnēs scīmus Marcum ad amphitheātrum īvisse.
3. Prō certō habēmus Titum sērō perventūrum esse.

Accusative and Infinitive (Indirect Statement) III

So far, the verbs of *thinking, knowing, saying,* and *seeing* introducing indirect statements have usually been in the present tense. Now look carefully at these sentences and compare them with the three sentences in Exercise 46a:

> Titus respondit sē domum redīre **nōlle.**
> *Titus replied that he was **unwilling** to return home.*

> Nōs omnēs sciēbāmus Marcum ad amphitheātrum **īvisse.**
> *We all knew that Marcus had **gone** to the amphitheater.*

> Prō certō habēbāmus Titum sērō **perventūrum esse.**
> *We were sure that Titus would **arrive** late.*

After the past tenses **respondit, sciēbāmus,** and **habēbāmus,** although the accusative and infinitive clauses are exactly the same in Latin as they were in Exercise 46a, in English

> the present infinitive is translated by *was unwilling,*
> the perfect infinitive is translated by *had gone,* and
> the future infinitive is translated by *would arrive.*

In all indirect statements, whether introduced by verbs in the present or a past tense,

> the present infinitive = action going on at the *same time* as the action of the main verb;
> the perfect infinitive = action that was completed *before* the action of the main verb;
> the future infinitive = action that will take place *after* the action of the main verb.

A sestertius of the Emperor Titus, with the Colosseum on the reverse. (Reproduced by courtesy of the Trustees of the British Museum)

Exercise 46b

Read aloud and translate each sentence, with the main verb first in the present tense and then in the past tense:

1. Titus spērat (spērāvit) puerōs ad mūnera itūrōs esse.
2. Marcus dīcit (dīxit) patrem epistulam cōnfēcisse.
3. Audiō (audīvī) Cornēlium ad Cūriam festīnāre.
4. Cornēlius dīcit (dīxit) sē Marcum sēcum ductūrum esse.
5. Num crēdis (crēdidistī) Cornēliam pūpā lūdere?
6. Prō certō habeō (habēbam) Aurēliam nōbīscum nōn itūram esse.
7. Aurēlia scit (sciēbat) Cornēliam pūpam filiae Dāvī dedisse.
8. Patruus meus respondet (respondit) sē manēre mālle.
9. Sextus dīcit (dīxit) Marcum domum mātūrē reditūrum esse.
10. Marcus putat (putāvit) sē numquam tot et tam variōs hominēs vīdisse.

Sōcratēs putābat sē esse cīvem tōtīus mundī. *Socrates considered himself a citizen of the whole world.* (Cicero)

Gladiators

Criminals sentenced to death could be purchased cheaply and thrown to the beasts or made to fight to the death, unarmed, in the arena. But those convicted of lesser crimes, for which the mines or deportation was the penalty, might instead go to a gladiatorial school. Slaves acquired through war or piracy were another source of recruitment, and occasionally volunteers, including Roman citizens, actually took up the gladiatorial trade. All gladiators bound themselves to their trade by an oath which laid down the severest penalties for backsliders or runaways: "to be burnt with fire, shackled with chains, beaten with rods, and killed with steel" (**ūrī, vincīrī, verberārī, ferrōque necārī**).

After thorough training in the barracks, the gladiator was ready for the arena. Successful gladiators, like chariot drivers, were popular heroes. This is an inscription from Pompeii:

> The girls' heart-throb, the Thracian Celadus, (property) of Octavius, 3 wins out of 3.

Victorious gladiators were richly rewarded and, after a period of service, might win the wooden sword of freedom, even if slaves. Veteran gladiators could also be employed as overseers in the gladiatorial schools.

The fate of a defeated gladiator rested with the spectators. If he had won favor, the spectators might wave their handkerchiefs, and the Emperor or presiding magistrate might then signal for his release. Otherwise, a turn of the thumb indicated that the fallen gladiator should speedily be killed.

There were various classes of gladiators—these included the heavily armed Samnite with oblong shield, visored helmet, and short sword; the Thracian carrying a small round shield and curved scimitar; the **murmillō**, or "fish man," who wore a helmet with a fish emblem on it and was armed with a sword and large shield; and the **rētiārius**, or "net man," who was unarmed but for a great net and sharp trident. Each had his own supporters: the Emperor Titus, for example, supported the Thracians, as did Caligula. Local rivalry, too, was common, as is borne out by this inscription from Pompeii:

> Luck to the people of Puteoli and all those from Nuceria; down with the Pompeians.

Such rivalry could lead to trouble, as this incident in the reign of Nero illustrates:

> About this time there was a serious riot involving the people of Pompeii and Nuceria. It started with a small incident at a gladiatorial show. Insults were being exchanged, as often happens in these disorderly country towns. Abuse changed to stone-throwing, and then swords were drawn. The games were held in Pompeii and the locals came off best. Many badly wounded Nucerians were taken to their city. Many parents and children were bereaved. The Emperor ordered the Senate to inquire into the matter and the Senate passed it on to the consuls. As a result of their report, the Senate banned Pompeii from holding any similar event for ten years.
>
> Tacitus, *Annals* XIV.17

Gladiātor in arēnā cōnsilium capit. *The gladiator adopts a plan in the arena.* (Seneca, *Epistulae Morales* XXII)

Nōn tē petō, piscem petō. Quid mē fugis, Galle? *It is not you I am aiming at, but the fish. Why do you flee from me, Gallus?* (spoken by the adversary of a **murmillō**; quoted by Festus, 285M, 358L)

Exercise 46c

Marcus reports back

Read the following passage aloud and answer the questions that follow with full sentences in Latin:

Marcus iam domum regressus omnia quae vīderat Sextō nārrābat:

"Cum amphitheātrō appropinquārēmus, vīdimus magnam hominum multitūdinem per portās intrāre. Nōs ipsī ingressī vīdimus multa mīlia cīvium iam cōnsēdisse. Ego nōn crēdidissem tot hominēs amphitheātrō continērī posse. Patruum exspectāre voluī, sed pater mihi dīxit Titum sine dubiō iam 5 adesse. Et rēctē dīxit; nam, cum ad locum magistrātibus reservātum vēnissēmus, vīdimus Titum eō iam ductum esse.

Subitō undique clāmātum est. Deinde vīdī prīncipem ā gladiātōribus salūtārī. Quam fortiter incēdēbant hī gladiātōrēs! Multī tamen eōrum moritūrī erant. Ubi pugnam commīsērunt, spectābam obstupefactus. Nihil tāle prius 10 vīderam. Vīdī multōs vulnerārī atque complūrēs quidem occīdī. Quam fortēs erant gladiātōrēs!

Maximē dolēbam quod ante merīdiem domum nōbīs redeundum erat. Titus dīxit sē mālle manēre, cum cuperet merīdiānōs vidēre. Spērō patrem mē ad amphitheātrum iterum ductūrum esse. Fortasse tē quoque dūcet." 15

crēdidissem, I would have believed   **pugnam committere,** to join battle
clāmātum est, there was shouting   **obstupefactus, -a, -um,** astounded

  incēdō, incēdere (3), **incessī,** to march

Exercise 46d

Respondē Latīnē:

1. Quandō Marcus hominum multitūdinem vīdit?
2. Quid Marcus vīdit postquam amphitheātrum intrāvit?
3. Quid Marcus nōn crēdidisset?
4. Quid Cornēlius Marcō dīxit?
5. Quem ad locum Marcus vīdit Titum ductum esse?
6. Quōmodo Marcus pugnam spectābat?
7. Quid Marcus in gladiātōrum pugnā fierī vīdit?
8. Cūr Marcus dolēbat?
9. Quid Titus dīxit?
10. Quid Marcus spērat?

Accusative and Infinitive (Indirect Statement) IV

Passive infinitives are also used in this construction:

Vīdī multōs **vulnerārī** atque complūrēs quidem **occīdī.**
I saw that many **were being wounded** *and several actually* **were being
killed.**

The present passive infinitive is already familiar from Chapter 29. It can be
recognized by the ending **-rī** in the 1st, 2nd, and 4th conjugations and the
ending **-ī** in the 3rd conjugation.

For the perfect tense, the passive infinitive consists of the perfect passive
participle and **esse.**

Vīdimus Titum eō iam **ductum esse.**
We saw that Titus **had** *already* **been taken** *there.*

Note that the perfect passive participle in this sentence agrees in gender,
case, and number with the subject of the infinitive, **Titum.**

Exercise 46e

Read aloud and translate:

1. Eucleidēs vīdit Cornēliam ā puerīs vexārī.
2. Sextus nescīvit vōcem suam audītam esse.
3. Vīdimus complūrēs nāvēs iam dēlētās esse.
4. Putāvērunt vestīmenta ā servō custōdīrī.
5. Scīvī mīlitēs in Britanniam mittī.
6. Fūrēs scīvērunt sē in apodytēriō cōnspectōs esse.

55

VERBS: Infinitives

You have now met the following forms of the infinitive:

	PRESENT		PERFECT	
	Active	Passive	Active	Passive
1	portāre	portārī	portāvisse	portātus, -a, -um esse
2	movēre	movērī	mōvisse	mōtus, -a, -um esse
3	mittere	mittī	mīsisse	missus, -a, -um esse
4	audīre	audīrī	audīvisse	audītus, -a, -um esse

	FUTURE
	Active
1	portātūrus, -a, -um esse
2	mōtūrus, -a, -um esse
3	missūrus, -a, -um esse
4	audītūrus, -a, -um esse

Deponent Verbs

The present and perfect infinitives of deponent verbs are passive in form; the future infinitive is active in form. For example,

PRESENT	PERFECT	FUTURE
cōnārī	cōnātus, -a, -um esse	cōnātūrus, -a, -um esse
sequī	secūtus, -a, -um esse	secūtūrus, -a, -um esse

Notes

1. The infinitives of 3rd conjugation verbs in -iō are not listed in the charts above because they are formed in the same way as the infinitives of mittō that are given.

2. The future passive infinitive rarely appears in Latin and will not be taught in this course.

3. Translations of the various forms of the infinitive are not given in the charts above because they will vary according to the use of the infinitive in the sentence. The infinitives of deponent verbs in all three tenses are active in meaning.

Graffiti and Inscriptions on Gladiators

Written at night on the facade of a private house in Pompeii:

D. Lucrētī Satrī Valentis flāminis Nerōnis Caesaris Aug. filī perpetuī
gladiātōrum paria XX et D. Lucrētiō Valentis filī glad. paria X, pug.
Pompēīs VI V IV III pr. Īdūs Apr. Vēnātiō legitima et vēla erunt.

*Twenty pairs of gladiators provided by Decimus Lucretius Satrius Valens
priest for life of Nero, son of Caesar Augustus, and ten pairs of gladiators
provided by the son of Decimus Lucretius Valens, will fight at Pompeii
on April 8, 9, 10, 11, and 12. There will be a regular hunt and awnings.*

Scratched on the columns in the peristyle of a private house in Pompeii:

Suspīrium puellārum Tr. Celadus Oct. III III.

*The girls' heart-throb, the Thracian Celadus, (property) of Octavius, 3
wins out of 3.*

A curse against a **bēstiārius**:

**Occīdite extermināte vulnerāte Gallicum, quem peperit Prīma, in istā
hōrā in amphiteātrī corōnā. Oblīgā illī pedēs membra sēnsūs medullam;
oblīgā Gallicum, quem peperit Prīma, ut neque ursum neque taurum
singulīs plāgīs occīdat neque bīnīs plāgīs occīdat neque ternīs plāgīs
occīdat taurum ursum; per nōmen deī vīvī omnipotentis ut perficiātis;
iam iam citō citō allīdat illum ursus et vulneret illum.**

*Kill, destroy, wound Gallicus whom Prima bore, in this hour, in the ring
of the amphitheater. Bind his feet, his limbs, his senses, his marrow; bind
Gallicus whom Prima bore, so that he may slay neither bear nor bull with
single blows, nor slay (them) with double blows, nor slay with triple blows
bear (or) bull; in the name of the living omnipotent god may you accomplish
(this); now, now, quickly, quickly let the bear smash him and wound him.*

Sepulchral inscription of a **rētiārius**:

**D. M. Vītālis invictī rētiārī, nātiōne Bataus, hīc suā virtūte pariter cum
adversāriō dēcidit, alacer fu. pugnīs III. Convīctor eius fēcit.**

*To the deified spirits of Vitalis, a net-fighter who was never beaten; a
Batavian by birth, he fell together with his opponent as a result of his own
valor; he was a keen competitor in his 3 fights. His messmate erected (this
monument).*

Versiculī: *"Hermes the Gladiator," pages 118–119*

Other Shows in the Arena

The Emperor Titus also held a sea fight (**naumachia**) on the old artificial lake of Augustus and afterwards used the empty basin of the lake for still more gladiatorial bouts and a wild-beast hunt (**vēnātiō**) in which over 5,000 animals of different kinds died in a single day. His brother and imperial successor, Domitian, was not to be outdone; he even used the Colosseum itself as a lake! Suetonius, in his life of Domitian, writes:

> Domitian constantly gave lavish entertainments both in the Amphitheater and in the Circus. As well as the usual races with two-horse and four-horse chariots, he put on two battles, one with infantry and one with cavalry; he also exhibited a naval battle in his amphitheater. He gave hunts of wild beasts and gladiatorial fights at night by torchlight, and even fights between women.
>
> He staged sea battles with almost full-sized fleets. For these he had a pool dug near the Tiber and seats built around it. He even went on watching these events in torrential rain.

Suetonius, *Domitian* 4

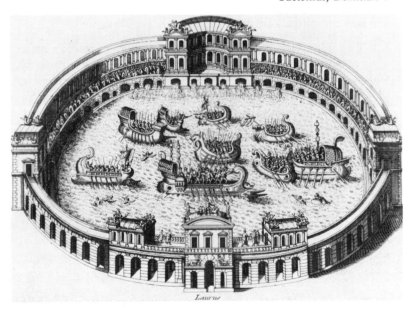

A drawing of a sea fight staged in an arena. Notice the rams on the front of the boats. (Photograph: The Mansell Collection).

Gladiators were not used to fight animals (bēstiae) in the wild-beast hunts. For this, special fighters, bēstiāriī, were employed. In these shows, such animals as lions, tigers, bears, bulls, hippopotami, elephants, crocodiles, deer, pigs, and even ostriches were made to fight each other or the bēstiāriī, or else driven to attack condemned criminals, who were sometimes chained or nailed to stakes. When Trajan held four months of festivities to celebrate his Dacian wars, some 10,000 gladiators and over 11,000 animals appeared in the arena over this period.

Vēnātiō

Even before the time of the emperors we read of the provinces being scoured for animals for these shows. Caelius, in a letter to his friend Cicero, wrote:

> Curio is very generous to me and has put me under an obligation; for if he had not given me the animals which had been shipped from Africa for his own games, I would not have been able to continue with mine. But, as I must go on, I should be glad if you would do your best to let me have some animals from your province—I am continually making this request.
>
> Cicero, *Epistulae ad Familiares* VIII.8

47
Androcles
and the Lion

Ōlim in Circō Maximō lūdus bēstiārius populō dabātur. Omnēs spectātōribus admīrātiōnī fuērunt leōnēs, sed ūnus ex eīs vidēbātur saevissimus.
Ad pugnam bēstiāriam introductus erat inter complūrēs servus quīdam cui
Androclēs nōmen fuit. Quem cum ille leō procul vīdisset, subitō quasi
admīrāns stetit ac deinde lentē et placidē hominī appropinquābat. Tum 5
caudam clēmenter et blandē movēns, manūs hominis, prope iam metū
exanimātī, linguā lambit. Androclēs, animō iam recuperātō, leōnem atten-
tius spectāvit. Tum, quasi mūtuā recognitiōne factā, laetī ibi stābant et
homō et leō.
Ea rēs tam mīrābilis turbam maximē excitāvit. Androclem ad pulvīnar 10
arcessītum rogāvit Caesar cūr ille saevissimus leō eī sōlī pepercisset. Tum
Androclēs rem mīrābilem nārrāvit:

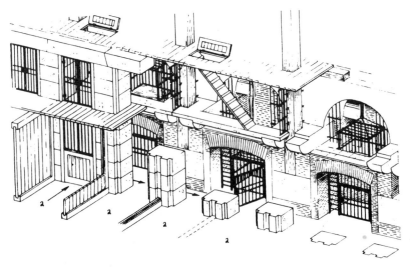

This diagram shows the cages for wild animals under the floor of the Colosseum. The animals
were brought in through an entry (marked a). The cages were hoisted to a higher floor directly
below the arena and from there the animals were driven up a gangway and into the arena
through a hatch.

"Dum ego in Āfricā cum dominō meō habitō," inquit, "propter eius crūdēlitātem fugere coāctus in spēluncam cōnfūgī. Haud multō post ad eandem spēluncam vēnit hic leō gemēns et dolēns, ūnō pede claudus. Atque 15 prīmō quidem terrōris plēnus latēbam. Sed leō, cum mē cōnspexisset, mītis et mānsuētus appropinquāvit atque pedem mihi ostendit, quasi auxilium petēns. Stirpem ingentem, quae in eius pede haerēbat, ego extrāxī ac iam sine magnō timōre vulnus lāvī. Tum ille, pede in manibus meīs positō, recubuit et dormīvit. Trēs annōs ego et leō in eādem spēluncā habitābāmus, 20 eōdem cibō vescentēs. Posteā captus ā mīlitibus, reductus sum ad dominum quī mē statim ad bēstiās condemnāvit."

Prīnceps, fābulā servī audītā, maximē admīrābātur. Androclēs omnium cōnsēnsū līberātus est, datusque eī leō.

admīrātiōnī esse, to be a source of
wonder or surprise (to)
quasi, as if
placidē, quietly, tamely
clēmenter et blandē, in a gentle,
friendly way
metū exanimātus, paralysed with
fear
mūtuā recognitiōne factā, recog-
nising one another

crūdēlitās, crūdēlitātis (f), cruelty
claudus, -a, -um, lame
lateō (2), to lie in hiding
mītis, -is, -e, gentle
mānsuētus, -a, -um, tame
stirps, stirpis (f), thorn
omnium cōnsēnsū, by general
agreement

admīror, admīrārī (1), admīrātus sum, to wonder (at)
lambō, lambere (3), lambī, to lick
parcō, parcere (3), pepercī, (+ dat.), to spare
cōgō, cōgere (3), coēgī, coāctum, to compel, force
vescor, vescī (3) (+ abl.), to feed (on)

Building Up the Meaning VII

What to expect after the verb audiō, "to hear"

Look at the following sentences:

Audīvit cūr pater advēnisset.
He heard why his father had arrived.

Clāmōrēs servōrum audīvit.
He heard the shouts of the slaves.

Audīvit patrem ad urbem advēnisse.
He heard that his father had reached the city.

You will see that the sense after *heard* can develop in three different ways:

He heard why, who, what, how. . . .   *indirect question* (with verb in the subjunctive)

He heard something/someone.   *direct object* (accusative case)

He heard that. . . .   *indirect statement* (with accusative and infinitive)

When you meet **audiō**, you must expect one of these three possibilities:

1. **Audiō cūr, quis, quid, quōmodo** . . . : Translate straight on, e.g.:

   Audīvī quid dīcerēs.
   I heard what you were saying.

2. **Audiō** *accusative* . . . : Wait to see if there is also an *infinitive*. If there is no infinitive, the accusative is the direct object of **audiō**, e.g.:

   Audiō servōs.
   I hear the slaves.

   Audiō servōs in viīs clāmantēs.
   I hear the slaves shouting in the streets.

3. If there is an infinitive, insert *that* . . . and continue with the translation of the accusative, e.g.:

   Audiō servōs cēnam parāvisse.
   I hear (that) the slaves have prepared dinner.

The following verbs have to be treated in the same way:

sciō, I know   **videō**, I see   **intellegō**, I understand   **sentiō**, I realize

Exercise 47a

Read aloud and translate:

1. Puerī audīvērunt gladiātōrēs prīncipem salūtantēs.
2. Eucleidēs nōn sēnsit ubi essent puerī.
3. Marcus vīdit gladiātōrēs iam in arēnam intrāvisse.
4. Spectātōrēs nōn intellegunt cūr leō manūs servī lambat.
5. Cornēlius sciēbat locum magistrātibus reservātum esse.
6. Androclēs dīxit sē stirpem ē pede leōnis extrāxisse.
7. Pȳramus crēdēbat Thisbēn ā leōne occīsam esse.
8. Nōnne audīs illōs leōnēs strepitum maximum facientēs?
9. Ita vērō! Leōnēs audiō; sed cīvēs maiōrem strepitum facere videntur.
10. Cīvēs intellegēbant servōs saepe fugere cōgī.

Exercise 47b

Read aloud and translate:

1. Puer nesciēbat quot gladiātōrēs vulnerātī essent.
2. Androclēs dīxit leōnem ūnō pede claudum ad spēluncam vēnisse.
3. Scīvistīne bēstiās sub arēnā continērī? Ipse eās audīvī.
4. Cīvēs prō certō habēbant nūllōs gladiātōrēs effugere cōnātūrōs esse.
5. Cīvēs audīre cupiēbant cūr leō hominem nōn necāvisset.
6. Fūr nesciēbat sē ā Sextō cōnspicī.
7. Spectātōrēs vīdērunt leōnem caudam clēmenter moventem.
8. Androclēs nōn intellēxit cūr leō pedem sibi ostenderet.
9. Marcus audīvit patrem domō ēgredientem.
10. Spectātōrēs vīdērunt ūnum leōnem saevissimum esse.

quid pro quo *literally,* "something for something," *one thing in exchange for another*

Manus manum lavat. *One hand washes the other* or *One good turn deserves another.*

Ab aliō exspectēs alterī quod fēceris. *Expect (the same treatment from another) that you give to your neighbor.* (Publilius Syrus 2)

How do these sayings fit the moral of the story of Androcles and the lion?

Versiculī: *"Another Example of Caesar's Leniency,"* page 120.

A gladiator's helmet embossed with figures representing Rome and its provinces. (The Mansell Collection)

63

48
Audience Reaction

Scene I: In the Amphitheater

(Licinius Caeliusque, duo spectātōrēs in amphitheātrō sedentēs, inter sē loquuntur.)

LICINIUS:	Ecce! In arēnam veniunt gladiātōrēs! Scīsne quot sint?
CAELIUS:	Minimē vērō! Scīsne tū quot leōnēs, quot tigrēs adsint? Ego audīvī multōs leōnēs ingentēs ab Āfricā allātōs esse et sub arēnā in caveīs 5 tenērī.
	(Intrat Postumius quī sērō venīre solet.)
POSTUMIUS:	Videō prīncipem iam advēnisse et ā cīvibus salūtārī.
CAELIUS:	Ecce! Iam gladiātōrēs eum salūtant! Ēheu! Sciunt sē moritūrōs esse.
POSTUMIUS:	Tacēte! Audiō bēstiās! Vidētisne leōnēs in arēnam immittī? 10
LICINIUS:	Ecce bēstia immānis! Servō illī parvō numquam parcet! Iam pugnāre incipiunt. Euge!
POSTUMIUS:	Euge! At cōnstitit leō! Mīror cūr leō cōnstiterit!
CAELIUS:	Num crēdis eum rē vērā cōnstitisse? Prō certō habeō eum mox impetum ferōciter factūrum esse. 15
LICINIUS:	At videō leōnem lentē et placidē hominī appropinquantem. Mehercule! Vidēsne eum manūs hominis linguā lambentem? Sciō leōnem esse saevissimum. Nesciō cūr hominem nōn occīdat.
CAELIUS:	Vidēsne servum leōnem spectantem? Timēre nōn vidētur.
POSTUMIUS:	Videō servum ā prīncipe arcessītum esse. Mīror quid dīcat. 20

Scene II: Leaving the Amphitheater

LICINIUS:	Nōn poteram intellegere cūr leō impetum nōn fēcisset. Mīrum quidem erat spectāculum.
CAELIUS:	Audīvī leōnem ā prīncipe hominī datum esse.
POSTUMIUS:	Ita vērō! Sed ecce! Paetus venit. Salvē, Paete!
PAETUS:	Cūr hunc tantum clāmōrem facitis? 25
CAELIUS:	Hoc vix crēdēs! Vīdimus leōnem, bēstiam saevissimam, servī manūs lambentem! Nescīmus cūr manūs nōn dēvorāverit.
PAETUS:	Quid? Nōnne audīvistis causam? Leō ille sēnsit sē hominem anteā vīdisse. Homō prīncipī nārrāvit quōmodo stirpem ōlim ē pede leōnis extrāxisset. Nārrāvit sē et leōnem in Āfricā in eādem spēluncā trēs 30 annōs habitāvisse. Ubi captus est, putāvit sē numquam iterum leōnem vīsūrum esse. Nesciēbat quō leō īvisset.
POSTUMIUS:	Agite! Sērō est. Ēsuriō! Domum redeāmus. Fortasse vidēbimus servum leōnem per viās dūcentem.

cavea, -ae (*f*), cage
immānis, -is, -e, huge
rē vērā, really, actually

impetus, -ūs (*m*), attack
redeāmus, let us return

immittō, immittere (3), immīsī, immissum, to send in, release
incipiō, incipere (3), incēpī, inceptum, to begin
mīror, mīrārī (1), mīrātus sum, to wonder
intellegō, intellegere (3), intellēxī, intellēctum, to understand, realize

Versiculī: *"Androcles' True Bravery,"* page 121.

Gladiatorial Fever

Sometimes high-born Romans were so enthusiastic about the combats in the arena that they took part themselves as gladiators. The Roman poet Juvenal, and Romans generally, strongly disapproved:

There in the arena you have a disgrace to the city: Gracchus fighting not in the arms of a **murmillō** with shield and saber, for he scorns and rejects such equipment; nor does he hide his face with a visor. Look! It's a trident he sports; he shakes his trailing net in his right hand, casts, and misses. Then he holds up his naked face for all to see and runs frantically around the whole arena, easily recognizable!

Juvenal, *Satires* VIII.199–206

Opposition to the Games

Some Romans protested the brutality of these shows. Seneca writes about the midday "interval" between the morning and afternoon sessions. In this interval criminals were forced to fight in the arena until everyone was dead:

Cāsū in merīdiānum spectāculum incidī lūsūs expectāns et salēs et aliquid laxāmentī, quō hominum oculī ab hūmānō cruōre acquiēscant; contrā est. Quicquid ante pugnātum est, misericordia fuit. Nunc omissīs nūgīs mera homicīdia sunt. Nihil habent quō tegantur, ad ictum tōtīs corporibus expositī numquam frūstrā manum mittunt. Hoc plērīque ōrdināriīs paribus et pos- 5 tulātīciīs praeferunt. Quidnī praeferant? Nōn galeā, nōn scūtō repellitur fer- rum. Quō mūnīmenta? Quō artēs? Omnia ista mortis morae sunt. Māne leōnibus et ursīs hominēs, merīdiē spectātōribus suīs obiciuntur. Interfectōrēs interfectūrīs iubent obicī et victōrem in aliam dētinent caedem. Exitus pug- nantium mors est; ferrō et igne rēs geritur. 10

By chance I attended a midday exhibition, expecting some fun, wit, and relaxation—an exhibition at which men's eyes have respite from the slaughter of their fellow-men. But it was quite the reverse. The previous combats were the essence of compassion; but now all the trifling is put aside and it is pure murder. The men have no defensive armor. They are exposed to blows at all points, and no one ever strikes in vain. Many persons prefer this program to the usual pairs and to the bouts "by request." Of course they do; there is no helmet or shield to deflect the weapon. What is the need of defensive armor, or of skill? All these mean delaying death. In the morning they throw men to the lions and the bears; at noon, they throw them to the spectators. The spectators demand that the slayer shall face the man who is to slay him in his turn; and they always reserve the latest conqueror for another butchering. The outcome of every fight is death, and the means are fire and sword.

Seneca, *Epistulae Morales* VII

After Seneca, others came out against the institution of the games. Among these were Christian writers like Tertullian and Augustine. The Emperor Constantine made a decree of abolition but this seems not to have been enforced. Gladiatorial shows were finally suppressed by Honorius (Emperor of the West, A.D. 395–423), though other blood-sports in the arena contin- ued for several centuries after this.

66

Word Study XII

Suffixes -ārium and -ōrium

The addition of the suffix -ārium (neuter form of the adjectival suffix -ārius; see Word Study V) to the base of a Latin noun or adjective creates a 2nd declension neuter noun meaning "a place for . . . ," e.g., **libr-** (base of **liber**, *book*) + -ārium = **librārium**, -ī (n), *a place for books* or *a bookcase*. English sometimes uses this Latin suffix to create new words, such as *aquarium*, (literally, "a place for water," from Latin **aqua**); but most English words derived from Latin words with the suffix -ārium end in -ary, e.g., *library*.

Similarly, the suffix -ōrium (neuter form of -ōrius, an adjectival suffix similar to -ārius), when added to the supine stem of a Latin verb, forms a 2nd declension neuter noun which denotes a place where the action of the verb takes place, e.g., **audīt-** (supine stem of **audīre**, *to hear*) + -ōrium = **audītōrium**, -ī (n), "a place for listening," or *a lecture-room*.

Exercise 1

Give the meaning of each of the following Latin nouns, using the words in parentheses as guides. Confirm the meanings in a Latin dictionary.

1. caldārium (**calidus**)
2. repositōrium (**repōnere**)
3. armārium (**arma**)
4. aviārium (**avis**, *bird*)
5. sōlārium (**sōl**, *sun*)
6. Tabulārium (**tabula**, *tablet*, *record*)

Exercise 2

Give the meaning of each of the following English nouns, and give the Latin root word from which each is derived:

1. dormitory
2. infirmary
3. lavatory
4. terrarium
5. laboratory
6. diary

Suffix -ūra

The suffix -ūra may be added to the supine stem of a Latin verb to form a 1st declension noun which means the "act of or result of . . . ," e.g., **scrīpt-** (supine stem of **scrībere**, *to write*) + -ūra = **scrīptūra**, -ae (f), *a writing*. English words derived from these nouns generally end in -ure, e.g., *scripture*.

67

Exercise 3

Give the Latin noun ending in -*ūra* which is formed from the supine stem of each of the following verbs. Give the English derivative of each noun formed. Consult an English dictionary as needed.

1. colō
2. coniciō
3. adveniō
4. stō
5. pōnō
6. capiō
7. misceō
8. nāscor

Exercise 4

Give the meaning of each of the following English nouns and give the Latin verb from which each is derived. Consult an English dictionary, as needed.

1. lecture
2. creature
3. pasture
4. aperture
5. rupture
6. stricture

Suffix -*mentum*

When the suffix -*mentum* is added to the present stem of a Latin verb, a 2nd declension neuter noun is formed which means the "result of or means of" the action of the verb, e.g., **impedī-** (pres. stem of **impedīre**, *to hinder*) + -*mentum* = **impedīmentum**, -ī (*n*), *a hindrance*; plural, *baggage*. English derivatives of these nouns end in -*ment*, e.g., *impediment*. Latin nouns ending in -*mentum* frequently alter the spelling of the present stem of the root verb, e.g., **documentum**, from **docēre**.

Exercise 5

Give the Latin noun ending in -*mentum* formed from the present stem of each of the following verbs. Give the meaning of the noun and its English derivative.

1. compleō
2. ligō
3. paviō (4) *to pound, tamp down*

Exercise 6

Give the meaning of each of the following English words and give the Latin root verb from which each is derived. Consult an English dictionary as needed.

1. sediment
2. monument
3. sentiment
4. regiment
5. momentum
6. augment

Inceptive Verbs

Latin verbs which end in *-scō* are called *inceptive* (from **incipiō**, *to begin*) since they denote an action in its beginning stages, e.g., **conticēscō**, *to become silent*. Compare the simple verb, **taceō**, *to be silent*. Inceptive verbs are in the 3rd conjugation. Often the inceptive is related to a noun or adjective rather than to another verb, e.g., **advesperāscit**, *it grows dark*, from **vesper**, *evening*.

Exercise 7

Using the words in parentheses as a guide, give the meaning of each of the following inceptive verbs:

1. quiēscō (**quiēs, quiētis**, *f*, *rest, quiet*)
2. convalēscō (**valeō**, *to be strong*)
3. senēscō (**senex**, *old*)
4. ingravēscō (**ingravō**, *to burden: cf.* **gravis**, *heavy*)
5. aegrēscō (**aeger**, *sick*)
6. stupēscō (**stupeō**, *to be amazed*)
7. proficīscor (**faciō**, *to make, do*)
8. adolēscō (**adulēscēns**, *a young man*)

Exercise 8

The present participle stem of an inceptive verb often becomes an English word. Give the meaning of the following English words, derived from inceptive verbs in Exercise 7. Consult an English dictionary as needed.

1. convalescent   2. quiescent   3. adolescent   4. senescent

Review XI

Exercise XIa

Read aloud and translate. Identify each indirect statement, indirect question, ablative absolute, and circumstantial clause. Identify the tense and voice of each infinitive, subjunctive, and participle.

1. Sciēbāmus multōs fūrēs vestīmenta ē balneīs surrepta in urbe vēndere.
2. Pȳramus, vestīgiīs leōnis vīsīs, putāvit puellam necātam esse.
3. Thisbē, corpore Pȳramī vīsō, gladiō strictō dīcit ipsam sē occīsūram esse.
4. Ex urbe profectūrī audīvimus viam Appiam esse clausam. Nesciēbāmus quandō Bāiās perventūrī essēmus.
5. Puerī ex ātriō ēgredientēs, vōce Eucleidis audītā, sē in cubiculum cōnfugitūrōs esse mussāvērunt.
6. Sextus spērāvit sē suum patrem vīsūrum esse. Ē lūdō enim domum missus sciēbat Cornēlium sē pūnītūrum esse.
7. Titō rogantī Cornēlius respondit Aurēliam ad amphitheātrum nōn itūram esse; eam domī manēre mālle.
8. Marcus Titum cōnspectum rogāvit quot spectātōrēs amphitheātrō continērī possent.
9. Gladiātōrēs pugnātūrī Caesarem salūtāre solent. Sciunt multōs esse moritūrōs.
10. Post pugnās in amphitheātrō spectātōrēs multōs gladiātōrēs occīsōs esse vīdērunt.
11. Aurēlia servōs in culīnā loquentēs audīvit.
12. Cornēlia Valerium ad Italiam regressum esse nōn audīverat.
13. Spectātōrēs nōn audīverant cūr servus līberātus esset.
14. Stirpe ē pede extractā, leō recubuit et dormīvit.
15. Prīnceps, fābulā audītā, cōnstituit servō parcere. Negāvit enim sē umquam prius tālem fābulam audīvisse.
16. Audīvimus spectātōrēs, cum leōnem hominis manūs lambentem vīdissent, attonitōs fuisse.
17. Cornēlius putāvit Titum domum sē secūtum esse; sed mox intellēxit eum in amphitheātrō morātum esse.
18. Sextō vīsō, fūr effugere cōnāns in pavīmentō lāpsus est.
19. "Ēheu!" inquit Thisbē. "Putō meum vēlāmen tē perdidisse." Quibus verbīs dictīs, sē occīdere cōnāta est.

negō (1), to say that . . . not

70

Exercise XIb

Read the following passage and answer the questions below in English:

Tale of a Tyrant

Dionȳsius, ille Syrācūsānōrum tyrannus, ōlim dēmōnstrābat tyrannōs nōn semper esse beātōs. Nam cum quīdam ex assentātōribus eius, Dāmoclēs nōmine, dīvitiās eius et magnificentiam rēgnī commemorāret, "Vīsne igitur," inquit, "ō Dāmoclē, quoniam haec tē vīta dēlectat, ipse eam vītam dēgustāre?" Cum sē ille cupere dīxisset, Dionȳsius iussit hominem, pulcherrimīs ves- 5 tibus indūtum, in lectō aureō recumbere. Tum ad mēnsam puerōs pulcherrimōs iussit cōnsistere et eī dīligenter ministrāre. Aderant unguenta, corōnae; incendēbantur odōrēs; mēnsae cibō ēlegantissimō onerābantur. Fortūnātus sibi Dāmoclēs vidēbātur.

At Dionȳsius gladium ingentem, ā lacūnārī saetā equīnā aptum, suprā 10 caput illīus beātī dēmittī iussit. Quō vīsō, neque pulchrōs illōs puerōs neque ōrnāmenta aurea Dāmoclēs spectābat, neque manum ad mēnsam porrigēbat. Dēnique ōrāvit tyrannum ut sibi abīre licēret, quod iam beātus esse nōllet.

Hōc modō Dionȳsius dēmōnstrāvit nēminem esse beātum, cui semper aliquī terror impendeat. 15

Syrācūsānī, -ōrum (m pl), the citizens
   of Syracuse, a city in Sicily
beātus, -a, -um, happy, blessed
assentātor, -ōris (m), flatterer
dīvitiae, -ārum (f pl), riches
commemorō (1), to mention, comment on
dēgustō (1), to taste, have a taste of

ministrō (1), to attend to
ā lacūnārī saetā equīnā aptum,
   hanging from the ceiling by a
   horse-hair
dēnique, at last
ōrō (1), to beg

porrigō, porrigere (3), porrēxī, porrēctum, to stretch out
impendeō, impendēre (2) (+ dat.), to hang over

1. What was the tyrant's name?
2. What did he wish to demonstrate?
3. What is the first thing we are told about Damocles?
4. In the phrase **dīvitiās eius**, to whom does **eius** refer?
5. Translate the words in which Dionysius makes an offer to Damocles.
6. Did Damocles accept?
7. What did Dionysius order Damocles to do?
8. Name five things that suggest the luxury of the situation.
9. Translate **suprā caput illīus beātī.**
10. In the phrase **quō vīsō** to what does **quō** refer?
11. What put an end to Damocles' feeling of happiness and what particularly alarmed him?
12. What request did Damocles make?

13. With reference to the last two lines, express in your own words the lesson Dionysius was illustrating.
14. "Although he had built up a successful business, the threat of exposure hung over the escaped war criminal like the sword of Damocles." Explain the significance of the final phrase.

Exercise XIc

In the passage in Exercise XIb, locate the following in sequence:

1. Examples of indirect statement.
2. Infinitives used with the verb **iussit.**
3. Imperfect and pluperfect subjunctives.
4. An ablative absolute.

49
Nothing Ever Happens

Sōl caelō serēnō lūcēbat. Cantābant avēs. Nātūra ipsa gaudēre vidēbātur. Trīstī vultū tamen sedēbat Cornēlia sōla in peristȳliō. Sēcum cōgitābat: "Mē taedet sōlitūdinis. Cūr nēmō mē observat? Cūr mēcum nēmō loquitur? Pater tantum temporis in tablīnō agit ut eum numquam videam. Māter tam occupāta est ut mēcum numquam loquātur. Marcus et Sextus suīs lūdīs 5 adeō dēditī sunt ut nihil aliud faciant. Nōn intellegō cūr nūper etiam servae mē neglēxerint, cūr Eucleidēs ille verbōsus verbum nūllum mihi dīxerit. Ō mē miseram!"

Cornēliae haec cōgitantī, "Heus tū, Cornēlia!" clāmāvit Marcus quī tum intrāvit in peristȳlium. "Pater iubet tē in tablīnō statim adesse. Festīnāre tē 10 oportet."

Cornēlia, cum in tablīnum intrāvisset, vīdit adesse et patrem et mātrem, id quod erat eī admīrātiōnī et cūrae.

Tum pater gravī vultū, "Ōlim, Cornēlia," inquit, "Publius Cornēlius Scīpiō Āfricānus, vir praeclārissimus gentis nostrae, dīcitur inter epulās 15 senātōrum fīliam suam Tiberiō Gracchō dēspondisse. Post epulās, cum Scīpiō domum regressus uxōrī dīxisset sē fīliam dēspondisse, illa maximā īrā erat commōta. 'Nōn decet patrem,' inquit, 'dēspondēre fīliam, īnsciā mātre.' At pater tuus nōn est Publiō Cornēliō similis, nam ūnā cōnstituimus et ego et māter tua iuvenī cuidam nōbilī tē dēspondēre. Quīntus Valerius, 20 adulēscēns ille optimus, vult tē in mātrimōnium dūcere, id quod nōbīs placet. Placetne tibi, Cornēlia?"

Cornēlia adeō perturbāta erat ut vix loquī posset, sed tandem submissā vōce, "Mihi quoque placet," respondit.

Cui Cornēlius, "Crās aderit Valerius ipse." 25

73

sōl, sōlis (*m*), sun
serēnus, -a, -um, clear, bright
avis, avis (*m/f*), bird
mē taedet (+ *gen.*), I am tired (of)
observō (1), to pay attention to
adeō, so much, to such an extent
dēditus, -a, -um, devoted, dedicated
nūper, recently
Heus! Ho there!
tē oportet (+ *infinitive*), you must

id quod, (a thing) which
cūrae esse, to be a cause of anxiety
   (to)
gēns, gentis (*f*), family, clan
epulae, -ārum (*f pl*), banquet, feast
nōn decet patrem, a father should
   not
similis, -is, -e (+ *dat.*), like, similar
   (to)
iuvenis, -is (*m*), young man
submissā vōce, in a subdued voice

neglegō, neglegere (3), neglēxī, neglēctum, to neglect, ignore
dēspondeō, dēspondēre (2), dēspondī, dēspōnsum, to betroth, promise in
   marriage

Exercise 49a

Using story 49 as a guide, give the Latin for:

1. Cornelia's mother is so busy that she never talks with her.
2. Marcus and Sextus are so devoted to their games that they do nothing with Cornelia.
3. Cornelia does not understand why the slave-girls have neglected her.
4. She does not understand why Eucleides has said nothing to her.
5. Cornelia was so happy that she could scarcely speak.

Result Clauses

When you meet these words—

adeō, so much, to such an extent   tam, so
ita, thus, in such a way   tantus, so great
sīc, thus, in this way   tantum, so much
tālis, such   tot, so many

—you will often find the word ut later in the sentence meaning "that,"
followed by a clause indicating result, e.g.:

Adeō perturbāta erat ut vix loquī posset.
She was so confused that she could hardly speak.

Tam occupāta est ut mēcum numquam loquātur.
She is so busy that she never speaks to me.

74

A negative result clause is introduced by **ut** and uses **nōn**, e.g.:

Adeō perturbāta est **ut** loquī **nōn** possit.
She is so confused that she cannot speak.

The verb in the result clause is in the subjunctive and is translated into the equivalent tense of the English indicative. The verbs **loquātur** and **possit** in the examples above are in the *present subjunctive*.

VERBS: Subjunctive Mood II

The imperfect and pluperfect subjunctives were tabulated on pages 10–11. The following is the tabulation of the other two tenses of the subjunctive, the present and perfect:

Present Subjunctive

		1st Conjugation	2nd Conjugation	3rd Conjugation		4th Conjugation
				ACTIVE VOICE		
	1	portem	moveam	mittam	iaciam	audiam
S	2	portēs	moveās	mittās	iaciās	audiās
	3	portet	moveat	mittat	iaciat	audiat
	1	portēmus	moveāmus	mittāmus	iaciāmus	audiāmus
P	2	portētis	moveātis	mittātis	iaciātis	audiātis
	3	portent	moveant	mittant	iaciant	audiant

				PASSIVE VOICE		
	1	porter	movear	mittar	iaciar	audiar
S	2	portēris	moveāris	mittāris	iaciāris	audiāris
	3	portētur	moveātur	mittātur	iaciātur	audiātur
	1	portēmur	moveāmur	mittāmur	iaciāmur	audiāmur
P	2	portēminī	moveāminī	mittāminī	iaciāminī	audiāminī
	3	portentur	moveantur	mittantur	iaciantur	audiantur

				DEPONENT VERBS		
S	1	cōner etc.	verear etc.	loquar etc.	regrediar etc.	experiar etc.

esse		So also		īre		So also
1	si*m*	**possim**		ea*m*		**feram**
S 2	sī*s*	**velim**		eā*s*		**fiam**
3	si*t*	**nōlim**		ea*t*		
		mālim				
1	sī*mus*			eā*mus*		
P 2	sī*tis*			eā*tis*		
3	si*nt*			ea*nt*		

Perfect Subjunctive

		ACTIVE VOICE			
1	portāv*erim*	mōv*erim*	mīs*erim*	iēc*erim*	audīv*erim*
S 2	portāv*eris*	mōv*eris*	mīs*eris*	iēc*eris*	audīv*eris*
3	portāv*erit*	mōv*erit*	mīs*erit*	iēc*erit*	audīv*erit*
1	portāv*erimus*	mōv*erimus*	mīs*erimus*	iēc*erimus*	audīv*erimus*
P 2	portāv*eritis*	mōv*eritis*	mīs*eritis*	iēc*eritis*	audīv*eritis*
3	portāv*erint*	mōv*erint*	mīs*erint*	iēc*erint*	audīv*erint*

		PASSIVE VOICE			
S 1	portātus sim etc.	mōtus sim etc.	missus sim etc.	iactus sim etc.	audītus sim etc.

		DEPONENT VERBS			
S 1	cōnātus sim etc.	veritus sim etc.	locūtus sim etc.	regressus sim etc.	expertus sim etc.

IRREGULAR VERBS

S 1	fu*erim* etc.

So also **potuerim, voluerim, nōluerim, māluerim, īverim,** and **tulerim.** The perfect subjunctive of **fīō** is **factus sim.**

Be sure to learn the above forms thoroughly.

Sequence of Tenses

Compare the following pairs of sentences containing indirect questions:

1. a. Nōn intellegō cūr servae mē **neglegant**.
    I do not understand why the slave-girls neglect me.
   b. Nōn intellegō cūr servae mē **neglēxerint**.
    I do not understand why the slave-girls neglected me.

2. a. Nōn intellegēbam cūr servae mē **neglegerent**.
    I did not understand why the slave-girls were neglecting me.
   b. Nōn intellegēbam cūr servae mē **neglēxissent**.
    I did not understand why the slave-girls had neglected me.

When the verb in the main clause is in the *present tense* (as in 1.a and 1.b above), a *present subjunctive* in the indirect question (as in 1.a above) indicates an action going on at the same time as that of the main verb, and a *perfect subjunctive* in the indirect question (as in 1.b above) indicates an action that took place before that of the main verb.

When the verb in the main clause is in the *past tense* (as in 2.a and 2.b above), an *imperfect subjunctive* in the indirect question (as in 2.a above) indicates an action going on at the same time as that of the main verb, and a *pluperfect subjunctive* in the indirect question (as in 2.b above) indicates an action that took place before that of the main verb.

This relationship between the tense of the verb in the main clause and the tense of the subjunctive in the subordinate clause is called *sequence of tenses*. The sequence is said to be *primary* when the verb in the main clause is in a primary tense, i.e., *present* or *future* or *future perfect*, as in 1.a and 1.b above. The sequence is said to be *secondary* when the verb in the main clause is in a secondary tense, i.e., *imperfect* or *perfect* or *pluperfect*, as in 2.a and 2.b above.

PRIMARY SEQUENCE

Verb of Main Clause	Verb of Subordinate Clause
present, future, or future perfect indicative	present subjunctive (for action going on at the *same time* as that of the main verb) perfect subjunctive (for action that took place *before* that of the main verb)

77

Verb of Main Clause	Verb of Subordinate Clause
imperfect, perfect, or pluperfect indicative	imperfect subjunctive (for action going on at the same time as that of the main verb)
	pluperfect subjunctive (for action that took place before that of the main verb)

Sequence of Tenses in Result Clauses

In result clauses a *present subjunctive* will be used in primary sequence, and the *imperfect subjunctive* may be used in secondary sequence. (See the examples in the note on result clauses on pages 74–5.) In practice, however, the Romans were more flexible in choosing the tenses of result clauses, and fairly regularly the *perfect subjunctive* is found in result clauses after main verbs in *secondary tenses*. This puts a special emphasis on the result that took place.

Exercise 49b

Read aloud and translate each sentence, and then explain the sequence of tenses between the main and the subordinate clauses:

1. Tam laetae cantant avēs ut nātūra ipsa gaudēre videātur.
2. Leō tantus et tam ferōx erat ut servus metū exanimātus ceciderit.
3. Tot spectātōrēs ad lūdōs convēnerant ut Circus vix omnēs continēret.
4. Cornēliī filia adeō perturbāta erat ut submissā vōce respondēret.
5. Tanta tempestās coorta erat ut sērō Brundisium advēnerimus.
6. Cornēlia nōn rogāvit cūr pater sē Valeriō dēspondisset.
7. Tālis iuvenis erat Valerius ut Cornēliō placēret filiam eī dēspondēre.
8. Cornēlia tam laeta subitō fit ut omnia Flāviae nārrāre cupiat.
9. Cornēlia, "Tam laeta sum," inquit, "ut vix loquī possim."
10. Pater tam gravī vultū locūtus est ut Cornēlia mīrārētur quid accidisset.

Roman Weddings I

When a Roman girl reached marriageable age—somewhere between twelve and fourteen—her father set about finding her a husband.

When a friend asked the writer Pliny to help him find a suitable match for his niece, Pliny wrote back to say that a certain Acilianus would be just the man. After speaking highly of Acilianus' father, his grandmother on his mother's side, and his uncle, he describes the prospective bridegroom as follows:

> Acilianus himself is a person of very great energy and application, but at the same time exceedingly modest. He has held the offices of quaestor, tribune, and praetor with very great distinction, and this relieves you of the need to canvass on his behalf. His expression is frank and open; his complexion is fresh and he has a healthy color; his whole bearing is noble and handsome, with the dignity of a senator. I don't know whether I should add that his father has ample means; for, when I picture you and your brother for whom we are seeking a son-in-law, I think there is no need for me to say more on that subject; and yet, when I consider the attitudes of people nowadays and even the laws of the country, which judge a man's income as of primary importance, I'm probably right in thinking that even a reference to his father's means should not be omitted. Certainly, if one thinks of the children of the marriage and their children, one must take the question of money into account when making a choice.
>
> Pliny, *Letters* I.14

When we remember that a Roman would be nearly forty before he attained the praetorship, Pliny's candidate (if we read between the lines) was probably red-faced, stout, and middle-aged, but Pliny seems to consider these points less important than having good family connections and plenty of money.

So our thirteen-year-old Cornelia might find herself engaged to a mere boy (minimum age fourteen) or to someone three times her age, but she was not expected to raise any objections to what was simply a legal contract between families.

Before the actual wedding, a betrothal ceremony (**spōnsālia**) often took place, witnessed by relatives and friends. The father of the girl was asked formally if he "promised" his daughter and replied that he did. (Question: **Spondēsne?** Answer: **Spondeō.**) Gifts were then given to the bride-to-be, including a ring (**ānulus**) either of gold or of iron set in gold. This was worn on the third finger of the left hand, from which it was believed a nerve ran straight to the heart.

Usually, the two families had already discussed the terms of the dowry (dōs, dōtis, given by the bride's father along with the girl), which was returnable in the event of a divorce.

Exercise 49c

Omnia iam diū ad spōnsālia parāta erant, īnsciā Cornēliā. Valerius enim, cum prīmum Brundisī ē nāve ēgressus est, ad Cornēlium scrīpserat sē velle Cornēliam in mātrimōnium dūcere; deinde Cornēlius rescrīpserat sē libenter fīliam Valeriō dēspōnsūrum esse; tum Aurēlia Vīniam, mātrem Flāviae, invītāverat ut prōnuba esset. Ad spōnsālia igitur Valerius et Vīnia et Flāvia 5 Rōmam iam advēnerant.

Aderat diēs spōnsālium. Quīntā hōrā omnēs Cornēliī atque propinquī amīcīque in ātrium convēnērunt. Deinde, silentiō factō, Cornēlia vultū dēmissō ingressa in ātrium dēducta est. Tum Valerius, quī contrā Cornēlium in mediō ātriō stābat, eī, "Spondēsne," ait, "tē fīliam tuam mihi uxōrem 10 datūrum esse?"

Cui Cornēlius, "Spondeō."

Quō dictō, Valerius ad Cornēliam conversus ānulum aureum tertiō digitō sinistrae manūs eius aptāvit. Tum ōsculum eī dedit. Omnēs spōnsō et spōnsae grātulātī sunt. 15

ad spōnsālia, for the betrothal
prōnuba, -ae (f), bride's attendant
propinquus, -ī (m), relative
vultū dēmissō, with eyes lowered
ait, (he, she) says, said

conversus, -a, -um, having turned, turning
ānulus, -ī (m), ring
sinister, -tra, -trum, left
aptō (1), to place, fit

spondeō, spondēre (2), spopondī, spōnsum, to promise solemnly, pledge
grātulor, grātulārī (1), grātulātus sum (+ dat.), to congratulate

Sīqua volēs aptē nūbere, nūbe parī. If you wish a suitable marriage, marry an equal. (Ovid, Heroides IX.32)

80

The Ring Finger

Aulus Gellius, a Roman scholar and writer of the second half of the second century A.D., gives the following explanation of why the Greeks and Romans wore rings on the third finger of the left hand.

Veterēs Graecōs ānulum habuisse in digitō accēpimus sinistrae manūs quī minimō est proximus. Rōmānōs quoque hominēs aiunt sīc plērumque ānulīs ūsitātōs. Causam esse huius reī Apiōn in librīs *Aegyptiacīs* hanc dīcit, quod insectīs apertīsque hūmānīs corporibus, ut mōs in Aegyptō fuit, quās Graecī ἀνατομάς appellant, repertum est nervum quendam tenuissimum 5 ab eō ūnō digitō dē quō dīximus, ad cor hominis pergere ac pervenīre; proptereā nōn īnscītum vīsum esse eum potissimum digitum tālī honōre decorandum, quī continēns et quasi conēxus esse cum prīncipātū cordis vidērētur.

I have heard that the ancient Greeks wore a ring on the finger of the left hand which is next to the little finger. They say, too, that the Roman men commonly wore their rings in that way. Apion in his *Egyptian History* says that the reason for this practice is, that upon cutting into and opening human bodies, a custom in Egypt which the Greeks call ἀνατομαί, or "dissection," it was found that a very fine nerve proceeded from that finger alone of which we have spoken, and made its way to the human heart; that it therefore seemed quite reasonable that this finger in particular should be honored with such an ornament, since it seems to be joined, and as it were united, with that supreme organ, the heart.

Aulus Gellius, *Attic Nights* X.10

A betrothal ring.
(Reproduced by courtesy of
the Trustees of the British Museum)

50
Marcus Comes of Age

Coming of age was an important occasion for a Roman boy and it was
marked both by an official ceremony (**officium togae virīlis**) and by family
celebrations. The ceremony usually took place when the boy had reached
the age of sixteen but not on his birthday. It was common for it to be
celebrated at the festival called the **Līberālia** on March 17. It began with
the boy dedicating (**cōnsecrāre**) the lucky charm (**bulla**) which he had worn
since he was a baby and the toga with the purple edge (**toga praetexta**)
which boys wore. These he placed before the shrine of the household gods
(**larārium**) which was usually in the atrium of the house. From this time
on he wore the plain white toga (**toga virīlis** or **toga pūra**) indicating that
he was no longer a boy but a man. After the ceremony members of his
family and friends escorted him to the forum (**in forum dēdūcere**). There,
in the building where the public records were housed (**Tabulārium**), his
name was entered in the records (**tabulae**, literally, "tablets"). The official
ceremony was now completed, and the family entertained their friends at
a private celebration.

The time has now come for Marcus to assume the **toga virīlis**.

Iam aderat mēnsis Martius. Erat diēs Līberālium quō diē adulēscentēs
Rōmānī togam pūram sūmere solēbant. Abhinc complūrēs mēnsēs Marcus
sēdecim annōs complēverat; nunc togam virīlem sūmptūrus erat. Itaque
Cornēlius amīcōs clientēsque omnēs invītāverat ut eō diē apud sē convenīrent. Omnēs sciēbant patrem Marcī dīvitissimum esse; omnēs prō certō 5
habēbant eum optimam cēnam amīcīs datūrum esse.

Domus Gāī Cornēliī plēna erat tumultūs, strepitūs, clāmōris. Tot et tam variī hominēs eō conveniēbant ut iānitor, ab iānuā prōgressus, in ipsō līmine sollicitus stāret. Sī quis appropinquābat, eum magnā vōce rogābat quis esset et quid vellet. Aliōs rogābat ut in domum prōcēderent, aliīs praecipiēbat ut 10 in viā manērent. Nōnnūllī autem, quī neque amīcī Cornēliī erant neque

clientēs, domuī appropinquāvērunt, quod spērābant Cornēlium sē ad cēnam invītātūrum esse. Hī iānitōrem ōrābant nē sē dīmitteret; ille autem eīs imperābat ut statim discēderent.

Tandem, omnibus rēbus parātīs, Cornēlius tōtam familiam rogāvit ut in 15 ātrium convenīrent. Aderant propinquī; aderant multī amīcī; aderant plūrimī clientium; aderant omnēs servī lībertīque Cornēliōrum. Cūnctī inter sē colloquēbantur, cūnctī gaudēbant quod ad hoc officium togae virīlis invītātī erant.

In ātriō ante larārium stābat Marcus togam praetextam bullamque auream 20 in manibus tenēns. Sēnsit oculōs omnium in sē conversōs esse. Conticuērunt omnēs. Marcus prīmum togam praetextam atque bullam ante larārium dēpositās Laribus familiāribus cōnsecrāvit. "Nunc," inquit, "hās rēs puerīlēs hīc dēpōnō. Nunc vōbīs, ō Larēs familiārēs, haec libenter cōnsecrō."

Quō factō, pater servō cuidam imperāvit ut togam pūram Marcō indueret. 25 Deinde parentēs eum amplexī sunt et cēterī eī grātulātī sunt. Nunc Marcus, multīs comitantibus, in Forum ā patre est dēductus.

Quō cum pervēnissent, Marcō ad Tabulārium ductō, pater eōs quī comitābantur rogāvit ut extrā Tabulārium manērent. Ipse ūnā cum fīliō et paucīs propinquīs in Tabulārium ingressus est, nam ibi nōmen Marcī in tabulīs 30 pūblicīs erat īnscrībendum.

83

Quibus rēbus cōnfectīs, omnēs adstantēs Marcum iam ēgressum magnō clāmōre salūtāvērunt. Deinde cum Marcus omnibus grātiās ēgisset propter tantam ergā sē benevolentiam, omnēs domum Cornēliōrum rediērunt, nam Cornēlius multōs invītāverat ut apud sē eō diē cēnārent. 35

sūmere, to assume (i.e., put on for the first time)
invītāverat ut, he had invited (them) to
līmen, līminis (n), threshold, doorway
sī quis, if anyone
nōnnūllī, -ae, -a, some
ōrō (1), to beg
nē sē dīmitteret, not to send them away

imperō (1) (+ dat.), to order
Larēs, Larum (m pl), household gods
familiāris, -is, -e, (belonging to the) family or household
erat īnscrībendum, had to be registered
grātiās agere (+ dat.), to thank
ergā (+ acc.), towards
benevolentia, -ae (f), kindness

praecipiō, praecipere (3), praecēpī, praeceptum (+ dat.), to instruct, order
conticēscō, conticēscere (3), conticuī, to fall silent
amplector, amplectī (3), amplexus sum, to embrace
comitor, comitārī (1), comitātus sum, to accompany

Exercise 50a

Respondē Latīnē:

1. Quid iānitor rogābat ut aliī appropinquantēs facerent?
2. Quid aliīs praecipiēbat?
3. Quid iānitor imperābat eīs quī neque amīcī Cornēliī neque clientēs erant?
4. Quid Cornēlius servō cuidam imperāvit?
5. Postquam nōmen Marcī in tabulīs īnscrīptum est, quid Cornēlius adstantēs invītāvit ut facerent?

Exercise 50b

Using story 50 as a guide, give the Latin for:

1. Cornelius invited all his relatives, friends, and clients to come together at his house.
2. Some who were not friends of Cornelius were begging the doorkeeper not to send them away.
3. Cornelius asked his whole household to come together in the atrium.
4. Cornelius asked his friends and clients to stay outside the Tabularium.
5. When Marcus had thanked everyone, they all returned to Cornelius' house.

84

Telling to, Asking to: Indirect Commands

Compare the following pairs of sentences:

1. a. Aliōs rogat **ut** in domum prōcēdant.
      He asks some to go on into the house.

   b. Aliōs rogāvit **ut** in domum prōcēderent.
      He asked some to go on into the house.

2. a. Hī iānitōrem ōrant **nē** sē dīmittat.
      They keep begging the doorkeeper not to send them away.

   b. Hī iānitōrem ōrābant **nē** sē dīmitteret.
      They kept begging the doorkeeper not to send them away.

In these sentences **ut** is translated by *to*. **nē** is translated by *not to*.

In the story you have also seen **praecipiō** (I instruct), **imperō** (I order), and **invītō** (I invite) used to introduce **ut** clauses. Other verbs are also used in this manner, with **ut** and **nē** followed by the subjunctive, e.g.:

moneō (I advise, warn); **persuādeō** (I persuade); **hortor** (I urge); and **obsecrō** (I beg, beseech).

These subordinate clauses with the subjunctive, introduced by **ut** or **nē**, are called *indirect commands*.

Note that most of the verbs that introduce indirect commands are followed by a direct object in the accusative case, e.g.:

Aliōs rogābat ut in domum prōcēderent. (See above.)

The verbs **imperō** and **persuādeō**, however, are followed by the dative case, e.g.:

Coquō imperāvit (persuāsit) ut in ātrium venīret.
*He ordered (persuaded) **the cook** to come into the atrium.*

Another arrangement is also possible, e.g.:

Imperāvit (persuāsit) ut coquus in ātrium venīret.
He ordered (persuaded) the cook to come into the atrium.

In this latter case, "that" may be used in translation, e.g.:

He ordered that the cook come into the atrium.

A *present subjunctive* will be used in primary sequence (examples 1.a and 2.a above), and an *imperfect subjunctive* will be used in secondary sequence (examples 1.b and 2.b above).

85

Exercise 50c

In story 50, locate 9 subordinate clauses that express indirect commands.

1. Translate the sentences in which these indirect commands occur.
2. Tell in English what the direct command (or request) was or would have been that is being reported indirectly in each case.
3. Locate one example of a subordinate clause with *indirect questions* (rather than indirect commands or requests) in story 50, and tell in English what the direct questions were that are here being reported indirectly.

Exercise 50d

Read aloud and translate each sentence, identify the type of each subordinate clause, and then identify the tense of each verb in the subjunctive.

1. Cornēlius convīvās omnēs invītat ut in ātrium prōcēdant.
2. Tum Cornēlius Marcō imperāvit ut rēs puerīlēs Laribus cōnsecrāret.
3. Cornēlius Marcum togā pūrā indūtum rogāvit ut ad Forum sēcum proficīscerētur.
4. In Tabulāriō pater rogat ut nōmen Marcī in tabulīs pūblicīs īnscrībātur.
5. Cornēlius omnēs convīvās invītāvit ut apud sē cēnārent.
6. Tē ōrō atque obsecrō ut domum veniās.
7. Iānitor iam iānuam claudēbat: tam dēfessus erat ut dormīre cuperet.
8. Asellus iānitōrem vīsum rogāvit quid eō diē fēcisset.
9. "Tibi dīcō," inquit iānitor, "plūrimōs hominēs ā mē aut ad iānuam acceptōs esse aut dīmissōs."
10. "Nōlī ibi morārī," inquam, "nam dominus imperāvit ut iānua claudātur."

Note that in sentence 10 present time is clearly in the speaker's mind when using the verb **imperāvit,** "has ordered." When the perfect tense is used in this way, the sequence is primary, and therefore a present subjunctive is used in the indirect command.

Exercise 50e

Select, read aloud, and translate:

1. Nōlī mē hortārī ut ad illam urbem (īrem/eam).
2. Tē semper moneō nē in mediā viā (ambulēs/ambulārēs).
3. Abhinc multōs mēnsēs Valerius Cornēliō persuāsit ut Cornēliam sibi (spondēret/spondeat).
4. Plūrimī hominēs domum Cornēliī pervenientēs rogābant ut intrāre (possint/possent).

5. Prīmō omnēs hominēs hortor ut in viā (maneant/manērent).
6. Deinde amīcōs propinquōsque Cornēliī rogāvī ut (intrārent/intrent).
7. Clientibus praecēpī nē statim in domum (prōcēderent/prōcēdant).
8. Nōnnūllī, quōs nōn prius vīdī, mē ōrant nē sē (dīmitterem/dīmittam).
9. Eōs monuī nē ad iānuam (morārentur/morentur).
10. Tandem coāctus sum servōs rogāre ut eōs baculīs (repellant/repellerent).

Ego vōs hortor tantum possum ut amīcitiam omnibus rēbus hūmānīs antepōnātis. *As much as I am able, I urge you to set friendship before all other human affairs.* (Cicero, *On Friendship* V.17)

Cicero: Coming of Age Ceremonies for Nephew and Son

When Cicero, the great statesman and orator (106-43 B.C.), was governor of Cilicia, an area of southern Asia Minor, he wrote the following in a letter to his friend Atticus (50 B.C.) about his nephew Quintus and his son Marcus:

Cicerōnēs puerī amant inter sē, discunt, exercentur, sed alter frēnīs eget, alter calcāribus. Quīntō togam pūram Līberālibus cōgitābam dare; mandāvit enim pater.

My son and nephew are fond of one another, learn their lessons, and take their exercise together; but the one needs the rein and the other the spur. I intend to celebrate Quintus' coming of age on the feast of Bacchus. His father asked me to do this.

Cicero, *Letters to Atticus* VI.1

The following year Cicero planned to give the **toga pūra** to his own son, Marcus, in his hometown of Arpinum to the south-east of Rome:

Volō Cicerōnī meō togam pūram dare, Arpīnī putō.

I wish to celebrate my son's coming of age. Arpinum, I think, will be the place.

Cicero, *Letters to Atticus* IX.17

On 31 March, 49 B.C., Cicero, barred from Rome for political reasons, wrote with pride from Arpinum:

Ego meō Cicerōnī, quoniam Rōmā carēmus, Arpīnī potissimum togam pūram dedī, idque mūnicipibus nostrīs fuit grātum.

Since Rome was out of bounds, I celebrated my son's coming of age at Arpinum in preference to any other place, and so doing delighted my fellow-townsmen.

Cicero, *Letters to Atticus* IX.19

Versiculī: "Nucēs Relinquere," pages 121–122.

Augury

Like the ancient Greeks, the Romans laid great stress upon augury, the "science" of "taking the omens." They would not contemplate taking any important step until it was clear from the omens that the gods were in favor of it.

First of all, they would offer a sacrifice to some appropriate god or gods. For example, for an important family event, they would offer a sacrifice to their household gods, called the **Larēs** and **Penātēs**, at the family shrine in the **ātrium**; someone planning to go on a journey might offer a sacrifice to Mercury, a soldier going into battle a sacrifice to Mars or Mithras, and a young man in love an offering to Venus or Fortuna. The Romans worshiped many gods, both native and foreign; all of them would have their own temples, each with a sacrificial altar outside in the open air.

At home, the sacrifice could be small cakes, honey, cheese, or fruit which would be burnt upon the altar. At a temple, an animal such as a pig, a sheep, or a bull (or all three, the **suovetaurīlia**) would be sacrificed.

In the latter case, once the animal had been killed, the vital organs—heart, liver, and intestines—were inspected by the **haruspicēs**, who claimed to be able to tell from the spots or marks on these organs whether the omens were favorable or not. If the omens were bad, the ordinary Roman simply put off the undertaking to another day. More sceptical Romans usually dismissed all this as mumbo-jumbo and, in fact, the Elder Cato said, "How can one **haruspex** look at another without laughing?"

The most popular form of augury, **auspicium** ("taking the auspices"), can be described quite accurately as "bird watching" (from **avis**, a bird, and **spectāre**, to watch). The **auspex** based his predictions upon the number of birds seen at a particular time, the direction of flight, and so on. Astrology, dreams, thunder and lightning, and strange events of any kind were all taken very seriously by those engaged in augury.

A procession on its way to the altar to sacrifice a pig, a sheep, and a bull. (The Mansell Collection)

How Numa Pompilius Became the Second King of Rome (715-673 B.C.)

The senators unanimously voted to offer the kingship to Numa Pompilius. When he was summoned to Rome, he ordered that, just as Romulus had obeyed the augural omens in building his city and assuming regal power, so the gods should be consulted in his case, too. Accordingly, an augur conducted him to the citadel and arranged for him to sit down on a stone, facing the south. The augur seated himself on Numa's left, with his head covered, and holding in his right hand the crooked staff with no knots which they call a **lituus**. Then, looking out over the city and the fields beyond, the augur prayed to the gods and marked off the heavens by a line from east to west, designating as "right" the regions to the south, as "left" those to the north, and fixing in his mind a landmark opposite to him and as far away as the eye could see. Next, shifting the crook to his left hand and laying his right hand on Numa's head, the augur made the following prayer: "Father Jupiter, if it is Heaven's will that this man Numa Pompilius, whose head I am touching, should be king of Rome, show us unmistakable signs within those limits which I have set." He then specified the auspices which he desired should be sent, and upon their appearance Numa was declared king and so descended from the augural station.

Livy, I.18

On the Importance of Consulting the Auspices

In ancient times scarcely any matter out of the ordinary was undertaken, even in private life, without first consulting the auspices. Clear proof of this is seen even at the present time by our custom of having "nuptial auspices," though they have lost their former religious significance and only preserve the name.

Cicero, *On Divination* I.16

Auspex with **lituus**

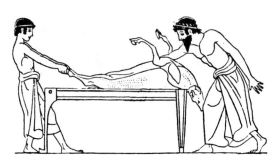

Haruspex with sacrificial victim

51
Papirius Praetextatus

Now that Marcus has assumed the **toga virīlis**, Cornelius will begin to consider his public career. In the early Republic, boys began their training for public life when they were much younger than Marcus is now. In those days fathers took their sons with them while they carried out their public duties. This story shows that Papirius, though still wearing the **toga praetexta**, had already learned how to be discreet.

Mōs anteā senātōribus Rōmae fuit in Cūriam cum praetextātīs filiīs intrōīre. Ōlim in senātū rēs maior agēbātur et in diem posterum prōlāta est. Placuit nē quis eam rem ēnūntiāret. Māter Papīriī, puerī quī cum parente suō in Cūriā fuerat, rogāvit filium quid in senātū patrēs ēgissent. Puer tamen respondit nōn licēre eam rem ēnūntiāre. Eō magis mulier audīre cupiēbat; 5 silentium puerī animum eius adeō incitāvit ut vehementius quaereret.

Tum puer, mātre urgente, prūdēns cōnsilium cēpit. Dīxit āctum esse in senātū utrum ūnus vir duās uxōrēs habēret an ūna uxor duōs virōs. Hoc ubi illa audīvit, domō trepidāns ēgressa est. Ad cēterās mātrōnās rem pertulit. Vēnit ad senātum postrīdiē mātrōnārum caterva. Lacrimantēs atque ob- 10 secrantēs ōrāvērunt ut ūna uxor duōs virōs habēret potius quam ut ūnus vir duās uxōrēs. Senātōrēs ingredientēs in Cūriam mīrābantur quid mātrōnae vellent. Puer Papīrius in medium prōgressus nārrāvit quid māter audīre cupīvisset et quid ipse mātrī dīxisset. Senātus fidem atque ingenium puerī laudāvit ac 15 cōnsultum fēcit nē posteā puerī cum patribus in Cūriam introīrent praeter illum ūnum Papīrium. Puerō posteā cognōmen honōris causā *Praetextātus* datum est quod tantam prūdentiam praebuerat.

mōs, mōris (*m*), custom	**trepidāns, trepidantis,** in a panic
posterus, -a, -um, next, following	**caterva, -ae** (*f*), crowd
placuit, it was decided	**potius quam,** rather than
nē quis, that no one	**fidēs, fideī** (*f*), good faith, reliabil-
ēnūntiō (1), to reveal, divulge	ity, trust
patrēs, patrum (*m pl*), senators	**ingenium, -ī** (*n*), intelligence, in-
eō magis, all the more	genuity
dīxit āctum esse, he said that there	**cōnsultum, -ī** (*n*), decree
had been a debate	**cognōmen, cognōminis** (*n*), nick-
utrum . . . an . . . , whether . . .	name
or . . .	**honōris causā,** as an honor
habēret, should have	**praebeō** (2), to display, show

agō, agere (3), **ēgī, āctum,** (here) to discuss, debate
prōferō, prōferre (*irreg.*), **prōtulī, prōlātum,** to carry forward, continue
urgeō, urgēre (2), **ursī,** to press, insist

---

mōs maiōrum literally, "the custom of the ancestors," *inherited custom, tradition* (used respectfully of the old ways as a guide for present conduct)

Mōribus antīquīs rēs stat Rōmāna virīsque. *On customs and men of olden times the Roman state stands firm.* (Ennius)

Ō tempora! Ō mōrēs! *How times and customs have changed!* (Cicero, *Orations against Catiline* I.2; spoken by the orator in indignation over the open conspiracy of Catiline against the Roman state)

mōs prō lēge A *long established custom has the force of law.*

mōre suō *in one's own way*

nūllō mōre *without precedent, unparalleled*

Exercise 51a

Using story 51 as a guide, give the Latin for:

1. It was the custom for Roman boys wearing the **toga praetexta** to enter the Senate House with their fathers.
2. Once, the senators were debating a rather important matter.
3. It was decided that the matter should be put off until the following day.
4. The senators ordered that the matter not be revealed.
5. The mother of Papirius asked her son what had been debated by the senators.
6. The boy replied that he would not reveal the matter.
7. The boy's silence aroused his mother all the more.
8. At his mother's insistence, the boy revealed that the senators were discussing whether a husband should have one wife or two.
9. Upon hearing this, Papirius' mother left the house.
10. She discussed the matter with other matrons.
11. It was decided that a crowd of matrons should go to the senate the next day.
12. In a panic they begged that one husband should have one wife rather than two.
13. The senators wondered why the women were saying this.
14. Papirius revealed what he had said to his mother.
15. The boy's ingenuity aroused the senators so much that they made a decree that afterwards only Papirius could enter the Senate House with his father.
16. As an honor they gave him the nickname *Praetextatus*.

Roman Names

In the earliest days, most Romans had only two names, that of the clan or **gēns** to which they belonged (**nōmen**), and their personal name by which they would be addressed by relatives and friends (**praenōmen**). Later, as families divided, branches of the same **gēns** were distinguished by a third name (**cognōmen**), e.g.:

Gaius (personal name) **praenōmen**
Julius (name of **gēns**) **nōmen**
Caesar (branch of Julian **gēns**) **cognōmen**

The **cognōmen** frequently started off as a nickname given to one member of the family, and it was handed down to his descendants as part of their name even though the nickname did not apply to them personally, e.g.:

P. Ovidius Naso ("big nose")
L. Domitius Ahenobarbus ("bronze beard")
M. Junius Brutus ("the stupid one")
C. Licinius Calvus ("bald")

A few Romans, who had earned some special distinction, were granted a fourth name (**agnōmen**) which was usually connected with the event which had made them famous, e.g., Publius Cornelius Scipio, who conquered the Carthaginians in North Africa, was called Publius Cornelius Scipio Africanus.

It is usual in Latin to find the **praenōmen** abbreviated. This is not the same as our practice of giving someone's initials. In Latin each abbreviation stands for a particular **praenōmen**. The following list contains most of the **praenōmina** in common use:

A.	= Aulus	L.	= Lūcius	S(er).	= Servius
App.	= Appius	M.	= Marcus	S(ex).	= Sextus
C.	= Gāius	M'.	= Mānius	Sp.	= Spurius
Cn.	= Gnaeus	P.	= Pūblius	T.	= Titus
D.	= Decimus	Q.	= Quīntus	Ti(b).	= Tiberius

Women usually had no **praenōmen**, but only the feminine form of the **nōmen** of their **gēns**, i.e., the **nōmen** of their father. Thus Cornelius' daughter is called **Cornēlia**. Sometimes the adjectives **Prīma, Secunda** or **Minor**, and **Tertia** were added to indicate the order of birth.

94

Roman Weddings II

In spite of the unromantic pre-arrangements, the wedding itself was celebrated with great festivity by the families and guests. The second half of June was considered to be the luckiest time for a wedding. On the evening before her marriage, the girl dedicated her toys to the household gods to show that her childhood had ended, just as a boy dedicated his **toga praetexta** and **bulla** at the coming-of-age ceremony. At the same time, she received her **mundus muliebris**—the jewelry, perfumes, toilet articles, and attire of the grown-up woman.

On her wedding day the bride wore a **tunica rēcta** which was plain white and over it a cloak (**palla**) which was saffron-yellow, as were her sandals. Her hair was specially styled for the occasion, and over it she wore a bright orange veil (**flammeum**). Her attendant was a married woman (**prōnuba**). The bride's house, where the wedding ceremony (**nūptiae**) was performed, was also decorated for the occasion.

The bride and her family and friends assembled in the **ātrium** and received the bridegroom and his guests. The ceremony began with a sacrifice, usually of a pig, the entrails of which were carefully examined by the **auspex** to make sure that the omens were favorable. If they were unfavorable, the marriage was postponed. The ceremony also included the signing of the marriage contract (**tabulās nūptiālēs obsignāre**) by ten witnesses, the joining of the couple's right hands (**dextrās iungere**) by the **prōnuba**, and the repetition of the formula **Ubi tū Gāius, ego Gāia** by the bride. Then the guests all shouted, "Good luck!" (**Fēlīciter!**).

The ceremony was followed by a banquet and then, after nightfall, the couple prepared to go to their new home. The bridegroom pretended to carry off the bride by force just as the Romans once carried off the Sabine women. Then the bride and groom were escorted home by a procession of guests (**dēductiō**) carrying torches (**taedae**) and singing songs to Hymen, god of marriage. Some guests threw nuts (**nucēs**) to children for luck. On arrival at the house, the bride was carried over the threshold (**super līmen tollere**) to avoid an unlucky stumble.

95

Word Study XIII

Latin and the Romance Languages

Although Latin has influenced the development of many languages (including English, of course), there are five modern languages which are so universally derived from Latin as to be called "Romance" (i.e., Roman) languages. These languages are Italian, French, Spanish, Portuguese, and Rumanian. The following examples show clearly the relationship of the Romance languages to Latin:

Latin	French	Italian	Spanish	Portuguese	Rumanian
arbor, *tree*	arbre	albero	arbol	árvore	arbore
dulcis, *sweet*	doux	dolce	dulce	doce	dulce

Rome's conquering legions brought Latin to lands as far apart as Britain and Egypt. In those places with well-established civilizations, such as Egypt, Latin did not displace the native languages; when the Romans left, Latin left with them. However, in areas such as Gaul (France) where civilization in Roman times was relatively primitive, Latin took hold and became the language of the people. The Romans also sent many colonists to these less-developed and less-populated provinces, further insuring the dominance of Latin as the accepted tongue in these lands.

In the evolution of provincial Latin into the Romance languages, these major developments (as well as many others) took place:

1. In general, the importance of word endings (inflection) in classical Latin was greatly reduced in the Romance languages. Nouns were usually reduced to two forms: a singular and a plural, e.g., the French *homme*, *hommes*, from the Latin **hominem**; and endings such as those of the comparative and superlative of adjectives were often replaced by words meaning "more" and "most," e.g., the Latin **dīligentior** became in Italian, *più diligente*. (*Più* is derived from the Latin **plus**.)

2. The definite article developed from the demonstrative pronoun and adjective **ille**. For example, the Latin **ille lupus** became "the wolf" in each of the Romance languages, as follows:

French	Italian	Spanish	Portuguese	Rumanian
le loup	il lupo	el lobo	o lobo	lupul*

(*The article is attached as a suffix in Rumanian.)

3. Pronunciation developed separately in each language, diverging greatly from that of classical Latin, e.g., the Latin word **caelum** (*c* pronounced *k*) became *cielo* in Italian (*c* pronounced *ch*), and *ciel* in French (*c* pronounced *s*).

96

Exercise 1

Next to each number below are words of equivalent meaning from each of three Romance languages. Give the Latin word from which each trio of Romance language words is derived and give the English meaning. Consult a French, Spanish, or Italian dictionary, as needed.

	Italian	Spanish	French	Latin	Meaning
			NOUNS		
1.	acqua	agua	eau	_____	_____
2.	amico	amigo	ami	_____	_____
3.	libro	libro	livre	_____	_____
4.	lingua	lengua	langue	_____	_____
5.	madre	madre	mère	_____	_____
6.	ora	hora	heure	_____	_____
7.	pane	pan	pain	_____	_____
8.	tempo	tiempo	temps	_____	_____
9.	terra	tierra	terre	_____	_____
			VERBS		
10.	abitare	habitar	habiter	_____	_____
11.	amare	amar	aimer	_____	_____
12.	dormire	dormir	dormir	_____	_____
13.	scrivere	escribir	écrire	_____	_____
			ADJECTIVES		
14.	buono	bueno	bon	_____	_____
15.	breve	breve	bref	_____	_____
16.	fàcile	fácil	facile	_____	_____
17.	male	malo	mal	_____	_____
			NUMBERS		
18.	quattro	cuatro	quatre	_____	_____
19.	sette	siete	sept	_____	_____
20.	dieci	diez	dix	_____	_____

Exercise 2

In which of the following places is French spoken? In which is Spanish spoken? In which is Portuguese spoken? Consult an encyclopedia as needed.

1. Brazil
2. Haiti
3. Guatemala
4. Belgium
5. Madagascar
6. Angola
7. Quebec
8. Argentina
9. Switzerland
10. Mexico

97

52
Cornelia's Wedding

Ubi diēs nūptiālis vēnit, omnēs mātūrē surrēxērunt. Aurēlia Marcum Sextumque hortābātur ut festīnārent. Ancillae hūc illūc concursābant ut omnia parārent.

Flāvia et Vīnia, māter eius, iam diū aderant. Mox adveniēbant cēterī amīcī et propinquī. Appropinquantēs laetī vīdērunt iānuam et postēs vittīs 5 et corōnīs myrtī laurīque ōrnātōs esse. Domum ingressī in ātrium ductī sunt ubi Cornēlia, tunicam albam indūta, flammeum gerēns, eōs exspectābat. Paulō post clāmor rīsusque maximus audītus est. Valerius cum propinquīs amīcīsque suīs intrābat.

Cornēlia cum prōnubā ad āram stābat. Sacrīs rīte parātīs, auspex prōcessit 10 ut porcum sacrificāret. Deinde tabulae nūptiālēs obsignātae sunt. Vīnia prōnuba dextrās Valeriī et Cornēliae iūnxit. Valeriō rogantī, "Quid nōmen tibi est?" Cornēlia, "Ubi tū Gāius ego Gāia," respondit. Quō factō, cūnctī, "Fēlīciter!" exclāmābant.

Cēnā iam parātā, omnēs convīvae accubuērunt, atque optimam post 15 cēnam cōnsecūta est commissātiō hilaritātis plēna.

Iam advesperāscēbat. Cornēlia ad mātrem haerēbat; Valerius simulābat sē eam ē manibus mātris vī abripere. Mox illa domum novam multīs comitantibus dēdūcēbātur. Praecēdēbant quīnque puerī quī taedās ardentēs ferēbant; subsequēbantur cēterī rīdentēs et cantantēs; nucēs ad līberōs, quī undique concurrerant, coniciēbant. Cum domum vēnissent, nova nūpta super līmen sublāta est nē lāberētur. 20
"Quam fēlīx est Cornēlia!" exclāmāvit Flāvia.

vitta, -ae (f), ribbon
myrtus, -ī (f), myrtle
laurus, -ī (f), bay (tree), laurel
ōrnō (1), to decorate
albus, -a, -um, white
paulō post, a little later
āra, -ae (f), altar
sacra, -ōrum (n pl), sacrifice

rīte, properly
auspex, auspicis (m), augur, officiating priest
dextra, -ae (f), right hand
nova nūpta, bride
nē lāberētur, so she wouldn't stumble

iungō, iungere (3), iūnxī, iūnctum, to join
ardeō, ardēre (2), arsī, to burn
nūbō, nūbere (3), nūpsī, nūptum (+ dat.), to marry

Exercise 52a

Respondē Latīnē:

1. Cūr ancillae hūc illūc concursābant?
2. Quandō clāmor rīsusque maximus audītus est?
3. Quandō prōcessit auspex?
4. Cūr auspex prōcessit?
5. Quid Valerius rogāvit cum dextrae iūnctae essent?
6. Quid Cornēlia respondit?
7. Quid Valerius simulābat?
8. Cūr nova nūpta super līmen sublāta est?

Purpose Clauses

In addition to the uses of the subjunctive described on page 11 (circumstantial and causal clauses and indirect questions), pages 74–5 (result), and page 85 (indirect commands), the subjunctive is used with **ut** to express *purpose.* Here, it is usually most naturally translated by "to" or "so that." The corresponding negative, **nē**, can be translated in various ways, e.g., "so that . . . not," "in case," "to avoid," or "to prevent." For example:

Auspex prōcessit **ut** porcum **sacrificāret.**
The priest stepped forward to sacrifice a pig.

Super līmen sublāta est **nē lāberētur.**
She was carried over the threshold so she wouldn't stumble.

The imperfect subjunctive is used in secondary sequence (as in the examples above). The present subjunctive is used in primary sequence (as below):

Auspex prōcēdit **ut** porcum **sacrificet.**
The priest steps forward to sacrifice a pig.

Super līmen tollētur **nē lābātur.**
She will be carried over the threshold so she won't stumble.

Ut amēris, amābilis estō! *To be loved, be lovable!* (Ovid, *The Art of Love* II.107)

Lēgum omnēs servī sumus, ut līberī esse possīmus. *We are all slaves of law so that we may be free.* (Cicero, *Pro Cluentio* 146)

Cūr nōn mitto meōs tibi, Pontiliāne, libellōs?
nē mihi tū mittās, Pontiliāne, tuōs!

Why don't I send you my little books of verse, Pontilianus?
So that you, Pontilianus, won't send me yours! (Martial, *Epigrams* VII.3)

100

Exercise 52b

Read aloud and translate each sentence, identify the tenses of all verbs, and determine whether the subordinate clauses are in primary or secondary sequence:

1. Multī amīcī convēnērunt ut novae nūptae grātulārentur.
2. Iānitor baculum habet ut clientēs repellat.
3. Marcus ante Larārium stābat ut bullam Laribus cōnsecrāret.
4. Cavēte nē cadātis, amīcī!
5. Ancilla in cubiculum festīnāvit ut Cornēliae speculum daret.
6. Servus vestīmenta custōdit nē quis ea surripiat.
7. Flāvia Rōmam veniet ut Cornēliam adiuvet.
8. Eucleidēs per viās festīnāvit nē ā praedōnibus caperētur.
9. Pater Sextī Rōmam redībit ut fīlium sēcum domum dūcat.
10. Marcus ad Tabulārium dēductus est ut nōmen eius in tabulīs pūblicīs īnscrīberētur.

Versiculī: "Bridal Hymn," page 122–123.

A Noble Wife

There is much evidence to show that husbands and wives loved each other and lived as happily as if they had themselves chosen each other. When a bride repeated the words **Ubi tū Gāius ego Gāia** at the wedding ceremony, she was promising to be a faithful wife. The following story, adapted from Pliny (*Letters* III.16), tells us how Arria, during the illness of her husband, concealed the death of her son from him to avoid aggravating his illness.

Aegrōtābat Caecina Paetus, marītus Arriae; aegrōtābat et fīlius, uterque mortiferē, ut vidēbātur. Fīlius dēcessit, puer eximiā pulchritūdine et parentibus cārissimus. Huic Arria ita fūnus parāvit, ita dūxit exsequiās ut ignōrāret marītus. Praetereā cum cubiculum eius intrāverat, simulābat vīvere fīlium atque etiam convalēscere; ac Paetō saepe interrogantī quid ageret 5
puer, respondēbat, "Bene quiēvit; libenter cibum sūmpsit." Deinde cum lacrimae prōrumperent, ē cubiculō ēgrediēbātur. Tum sē dolōrī dabat. Tandem siccīs iam oculīs, vultū iam compositō redībat; atque dum marītus aegrōtābat, sīc lacrimās retinēbat, dolōrem operiēbat.

marītus, -ī (*m*), husband	**dūxit exsequiās**, (she) carried out
mortiferē, mortally, critically	the funeral rites
eximius, -a, -um, outstanding	**cum**, whenever
cārus, -a, -um, dear, beloved	**quid ageret**, how he was
fūnus, fūneris (*n*), funeral	**siccus, -a, -um**, dry

dēcēdo, dēcēdere (3), **dēcessī, dēcessum**, to die
quiēscō, quiēscere (3), **quiēvī, quiētum**, to rest
compōnō, compōnere (3), **composuī, compositum**, to compose
operiō, operīre (4), **operuī, opertum**, to hide, cover

Another Story about Arria

The culmination of Arria's devotion is described in the following story of her death, also told in the letter of Pliny (III.16), from which the passage above is adapted.

Many years later Scribonianus in Illyria took up arms against the Emperor Claudius, and Paetus took part in the revolt. Scribonianus was killed, and Paetus was captured and put on board a ship to be taken to Rome. When he was about to go on board, Arria pleaded with the soldiers to be allowed to go with him. "Surely a man of senatorial rank is entitled to have some slaves to prepare his food, dress him, and put on his shoes? I will do all of these tasks on my own." Her request was refused, however. She therefore hired a small fishing boat and followed the larger vessel. When they reached Rome, Paetus was condemned to death, but he was told that he might take his own life, if he wished. At that point, Arria, who had no desire to go on living after the death of her husband, drew a dagger, plunged it into her breast, drew it out, and, as she held it out to her husband, uttered the immortal words, **Paete, nōn dolet** ("Paetus, it does not hurt").

Martial wrote the following epigram on Arria's death:

Casta suō gladium cum trāderet Arria Paetō
   quem dē vīsceribus trāxerat ipsa suīs,
"Crēde mihī, vulnus quod fēcī nōn dolet," inquit.
   "Sed quod tū faciēs, hoc mihi, Paete, dolet."

Martial, Epigrams I.13

castus, -a, -um, virtuous, chaste
dē (+ *abl.*), (*here*) from
viscera, viscerum (*n pl*), the inner organs of the body, the womb

102

Roman Funerals

When a death occurred in a Roman family, it was the custom to display grief more than is common today. Tears and lamentations were expected, and it was usual, for female mourners at least, to beat the breast (**pectus plangere**) and go about with torn clothing (**scissā veste**) and dishevelled hair (**capillīs solūtīs**). Some families even hired professional mourners to do this for them.

In the case of an important family, like the Cornelii in our story, the actual funeral procession (**pompa**) was a very elaborate affair. After the body had lain in state, feet towards the door, in the **ātrium** of the house surrounded by lamps (**lucernae**) and candles (**candēlae**), there would be a procession through the city to the Forum and then on to the family tomb. It would be headed by trumpet players (**tubicinēs**) followed by the litter on which the body lay. Then, after professional mourners, singers of dirges (**nēniae**), and torch-bearers (a reminder of the days when all funerals had taken place at night), came members of the family wearing masks of famous ancestors (**imāginēs maiōrum**), and, in the case of a magistrate, even the public attendants (**līctōrēs**) carrying his symbol of office, the bundles of rods (**fascēs**). Family and friends followed. A halt was made in the Forum where a speech of praise (**laudātiō**) was made in honor of the dead man.

At the family tomb outside the walls, the body was usually placed on a funeral pyre (**rogus**) which was set alight by a member of the family after some of the deceased's possessions had been placed on it. Flowers and spices were also thrown on the fire.

After the body had been cremated, the ashes were cooled with wine and were collected with the bones in an urn and placed in the family tomb. The last farewell was then uttered, and after nine days of mourning a food offering was made at the tomb to the spirit of the dead man (**mānēs**).

Slaves and the very poor, who could not afford even to hire the four bearers to carry the bier, were usually buried in public cemeteries in simple coffins. Some, however, would join one of the guilds or societies that were formed to ensure a respectable funeral for their members and spare them the indignity of being flung into a common grave. The poor were buried on the day they died, and their funerals, like those of children, usually took place after dark with a minimum of ceremony. Death among children was common, both in the early vulnerable years and in later childhood, as is proved by many inscriptions found on tombstones in various parts of the Roman world.

53
A Sad Occasion

Mēnse Iūliō tantus erat calor in urbe ut omnēs ad vīllam redīre vellent.
Gāius Cornēlius igitur omnia parāre coepit ut Bāiās redīrent. Antequam
profectī sunt, accidit rēs trīstissima.
Cornēlius, ut solēbat, cum Titō frātre ad balneās īverat. Per tōtam domum
erat silentium. Subitō audītae sunt vōcēs atque clāmor. Cornēlius servōs 5
hortābātur ut lectīcam in domum maximā cum cūrā ferrent. Aurēlia, vō-
cibus audītīs, in ātrium irrūpit. "Quid factum est, Gāī? Cūr servōs iubēs
lectīcam in domum ferre?" Cui Cornēlius, "Titus noster aliquid malī accēpit. Frīgidāriī pavīmentum tam lēve et lūbricum erat ut ille lāpsus ceciderit. Putō eum coxam frēgisse. Medicus statim est arcessendus." 10
Multōs diēs Titus in lectō iacēbat. Prīmō convalēscere vidēbātur; mox
tamen fīēbat īnfirmior, nam in febrem subitō inciderat. In diēs morbus
ingravēscēbat.
Tandem tam īnfirmus erat ut vix loquī posset. Haud multō post ē vītā
excessit. Cornēlius maximō dolōre affectus est. Tōta domus sē dolōrī dedit. 15
Aurēlia et Cornēlia et omnēs ancillae, scissā veste capillīsque solūtīs, pectora
plangēbant. Corpus Titī, togā praetextā opertum, in ātriō in lectō fūnebrī
positum est. Circum lectum ardēbant lucernae et candēlae.
Postrīdiē corpus Titī summō honōre ēlātum est. Praecēdēbant tubicinēs.
Subsequēbantur in pompā virī taedās tenentēs, mulierēs nēniās cantantēs, 20
propinquī imāginēs maiōrum gerentēs, līctōrēs fascēs ferentēs; postrēmī incēdēbant familiārēs.

Cum in Forum vēnissent, Gāius Cornēlius prōcessit ut frātrem mortuum laudāret. Commemorāvit quālis vir Titus fuisset, quot merita in prīncipem cīvēsque contulisset. 25

Quō factō, corpus Titī ad sepulcra Viae Flāminiae in pompā lātum est. Ibi rogus exstrūctus erat. In rogum impositum est corpus et super corpus vestēs atque ōrnāmenta. Appropinquāvit Gāius Cornēlius taedam manū tenēns. Quam taedam oculīs āversīs in rogum iniēcit.

Exsequiīs cōnfectīs, Cornēliī trīstēs domum regressī sunt. Multa dē Titō 30 loquēbantur. Commemorābant quam hilaris fuisset, quantum līberōs amāvisset. "Maximē," inquiunt, "nōs omnēs eum dēsīderābimus."

lēvis, -is, -e, smooth
coxa, -ae (f), hipbone
est arcessendus, must be sent for
febris, febris (f), fever
morbus, -ī (m), illness
fūnebris, -is, -e, funeral
familiārēs, familiārium (m pl), close
  friends
commemorō (1), to mention, comment on, recount

merita cōnferre, to render services
  (to)
Via Flāminia, a road from Rome
  leading through the Campus
  Martius and north to Ariminum
  on the Adriatic Sea
hilaris, -is, -e, cheerful

hortor, hortārī (), hortātus sum, to encourage, urge
frangō, frangere (3), frēgī, frāctum, to break
ingravēscō, ingravēscere (3), to grow worse
exstruō, exstruere (3), exstrūxī, exstrūctum, to build

Exercise 53a

Using story 53 as a guide, give the Latin for:

1. In summer the heat is so great in the city that everyone wishes to return to the farmhouse.
2. Therefore Gaius Cornelius intends to prepare everything so that they may return to Baiae.
3. Cornelius as usual goes to the baths with his brother Titus.
4. "Watch out! The pavement is so smooth and slippery that you may fall."
5. Suddenly he urges slaves to bring a litter into the house.
6. Titus is now so weak that he can scarcely speak.
7. In the Forum Cornelius recounts how many services Titus rendered to the emperor and the citizens.
8. After the funeral the Cornelii recount how cheerful Titus was, how much he loved the children.

Statue of a man carrying funeral busts of his ancestors

106

An Account of Roman Funerals

The following account of Roman funerals was given by Polybius, a historian of the second century B.C.

Whenever an important citizen dies, they have a funeral procession, in which his body is carried into the Forum to the Rostra, sometimes upright so as to be conspicuous, less often in a reclining position. There, surrounded by the whole populace, a grown-up son mounts the rostrum and delivers a speech about the virtues and achievements of the deceased. As a result, the majority of those present are so deeply affected that the loss seems not merely a private one affecting the relatives only, but a public loss involving everyone.

Then, after he is buried with the usual ceremonies, they place a likeness of the deceased in a part of the house where everyone can readily see it, and they enclose it in a little wooden shrine. This likeness is a mask which reproduces with remarkable faithfulness the features and complexion of the deceased.

On the death of any important member of the family, these likenesses are taken to the Forum, worn by those members of the family who seem most nearly to resemble them in height and bearing. These people wear togas with a purple border if the deceased was a consul or praetor, totally purple if he was a censor, and edged with gold if he had celebrated a triumph or had any similar distinction. They all ride in chariots preceded by the fascēs, axes, and other emblems appropriate to the official positions held by each during his life; and when they arrive at the Rostra, they all sit down in their proper order on chairs of ivory.

It would be difficult to imagine a sight more inspiring to an ambitious young man than to see the likenesses of men who had once been famous for their goodness all together and as if alive and breathing. What sight could be finer than this?

Besides, the person who makes the speech over the deceased, after speaking of the deceased himself, goes on to tell of the successful exploits of the other ancestors whose likenesses are present, beginning from the earliest. In this way, by constantly refreshing their memories about the fame of good men, the glory of those who performed noble deeds becomes immortal, and the fame of those who served their country well is passed on to future generations.

Polybius, *Histories* VI.3

Epitaphs

Roman tombs ranged from the very simple to the extremely elaborate. There was usually an inscription on the tomb and many of these have survived. The following five are in some cases slightly modified. The fifth preserves the original spellings of the inscription.

(i)

Pontia Prīma hīc est sita. Nōlī violāre!

situs, -a, -um, buried   violō (1), to do harm

(ii)

Est hoc monumentum Marcī Vergileī Eurysacis pistōris redemptōris appāritōris.

pistor, pistōris (m), baker
redemptor, redemptōris (m), contractor
appāritor, appāritōris (m), public servant

(iii)

Carfinia Marcī līberta vīxit annōs XX. Iūcunda suīs, grātissima amīcīs, omnibus officiōsa fuit.

iūcundus, -a, -um, delightful
grātus, -a, -um, loved by, pleasing to
officiōsus, -a, -um, ready to serve, obliging

Funeral relief of Aurelius Hermia and his wife, a freedwoman.

(iv)

Dīs Mānibus. C. Tullius Hesper āram fēcit sibi ubi ossa sua coniciantur. Quae sī quis violāverit aut inde exēmerit, optō eī ut cum dolōre corporis longō tempore vīvat et, cum mortuus fuerit, īnferī eum nōn recipiant.

Dīs Mānibus, to the spirits of the dead
optō (1), to wish

eximō, eximere (3), **exēmī, exēmptum,** to remove

(v)

Hospes, quod deicō paullum est; astā ac pellege.
Heic est sepulcrum hau pulcrum pulcrai fēminae:
nōmen parentēs nōminārunt Claudiam.
Suom mareitum corde deilēxit souō:
gnātōs duōs creāvit: hōrunc alterum   5
in terrā linquit, alium sub terrā locat.
Sermōne lepidō, tum autem incessū commodō,
domum servāvit. Lānam fēcit. Dīxī. Abei.

cor, cordis (n), heart	**lepidus, -a, -um,** charming
(g)nātus, -ī (m), son	**incessus, -ūs** (m), bearing, walk(ing)
sermō, sermōnis (m), conversation, talk	**commodus, -a, -um,** pleasant

dīligō (dei-), dīligere (3), **dīlēxī, dīlēctum,** to love
linquō, linquere (3), **līquī,** to leave

Funeral Customs

Two Laws Concerning Burial

Law of the XII Tables:

Hominem mortuum in urbe nē sepelītō nēve ūritō.
No one must bury or burn a dead man in the city.

Law of the Colony of Julia Genetiva in Spain:

No person shall bring a dead person or bury one or burn one inside the boundaries of the town or the area marked around by the plough or build a monument to a dead person there. Any person breaking this law shall be fined 5,000 sesterces.

109

The Crier's Words at a Ceremonial Funeral

_____*, a citizen, has died; it is now time for those for whom it is convenient to go to his funeral. _____* is being brought from his house for burial.

(*name of deceased)

Building Up the Meaning VIII

Translating ut

You have now met the following uses of **ut**:

A. With an indicative verb, e.g.:

Semper, ut vidēs, negōtiōsus sum.
As you see, I am always busy.

Sextus, ut lupum cōnspexit, arborem ascendit.
When Sextus caught sight of the wolf, he climbed the tree.

Clue: **ut** followed by an indicative verb should be translated by "as" or "when."

B. With a subjunctive verb:

1. To indicate *result*, e.g.:

Tam īnfirmus erat ut vix loquī posset.
He was so weak that he could scarcely speak.

Clue: a word like **tam, tantus, tālis, tot,** or **adeō** suggests that the translation will be "so . . . that."

2. In an *indirect command*, e.g.:

Cornēlius servōs hortābātur ut lectīcam maximā cum cūrā ferrent.
Cornelius was urging the slaves to carry the litter very carefully.

Ōrāvērunt ut ūna uxor duōs virōs habēret.
They begged that one wife should have two husbands.

Clue: the **ut** clause depends on a verb of "telling," "ordering," "begging," "urging," "persuading," etc.

3. To indicate *purpose*, e.g.:

Gāius Cornēlius prōcessit ut frātrem mortuum laudāret.
Gaius Cornelius came forward to praise his dead brother.

This type of **ut** clause is very common after verbs which suggest that someone went somewhere *to do* something.

Exercise 53b

What would you expect **ut** *to mean in the following sentences?*

1. Cornēlius Cornēliae praecēpit ut . . . .
2. Tantus erat terror in urbe ut . . . .
3. Marcus, ut vidēs, est filius senātōris.
4. Iānitor servīs imperāvit ut . . . .
5. In urbem dēscendit ut . . . .
6. Aurēlia tam īrāta erat ut . . . .
7. Puerī ut vōcem patris audīvērunt . . . .
8. Senātōrēs nūntium mīsērunt ut . . . .
9. Sextus adeō ēsuriēbat ut . . . .
10. Eucleidēs, ut nōs omnēs scīmus, est ērudītissimus.

Exercise 53c

Read aloud and translate each of the following sentences, and then identify each use of **ut** *and explain the sequence of tenses for all subjunctives:*

1. Magister Sextō imperāvit ut domum statim redīret.
2. Sextus, ut imperāverat eius magister, domum statim rediit.
3. Marcus nōs rogat ut sēcum ad theātrum eāmus.
4. Puerī, ut Titum vīdērunt, eum laetī salūtāvērunt.
5. Amīcō meō persuāsī ut mēcum ad Circum venīret.
6. Eucleidēs, ut vōs omnēs scītis, fābulās puerīs semper nārrāre vult.
7. Servō imperāvī ut pānem emeret.
8. Cornēliī ex urbe Rōmā discēdent ut Bāiās redeant.
9. In balneīs paulīsper morābantur ut cum amīcīs colloquerentur.
10. Eucleidēs, "Ut fēriātī estis," inquit, "vōs moneō ut multōs librōs legātis."

111

At a Brother's Grave

The poet Catullus was very devoted to his brother who died far away from home in Asia Minor. Catullus visited the tomb and wrote these lines. He does not tell us what he sees for his brother beyond the grave. He merely seeks comfort from the age-old Roman ritual for the dead.

Multās per gentēs et multa per aequora vectus,
  adveniō hās miserās, frāter, ad īnferiās,
ut tē postrēmō dōnārem mūnere mortis
  et mūtam nēquīquam alloquerer cinerem.
Quandoquidem fortūna mihī tētē abstulit ipsum,   5
  heu miser indignē frāter adēmpte mihi,
nunc tamen intereā haec, priscō quae mōre parentum
  trādita sunt trīstī mūnere ad īnferiās,
accipe frāternō multum mānantia flētū,
  atque in perpetuum, frāter, avē atque valē!   10

gentēs, peoples
aequora, seas
vectus, having been carried, having traveled
īnferiae, -ārum (*f pl*), offerings and rites in honor of the dead at the tomb
dōnō (1), to present
mūnus, mūneris (*n*), gift, service
mūtus, -a, -um, silent
nēquīquam, in vain
cinis, cineris (*m*), ashes, dust (of the cremated body)
5 **quandoquidem,** since
tētē = emphatic **tē**
indignē, undeservedly
priscus, -a, -um, of olden times, ancient
   priscō . . . mōre, by the ancient custom
trīstī mūnere, through (my) sad service (to the dead)
multum, abundantly
mānantia flētū, flowing with tears
10 **in perpetuum,** forever

Versiculī: *"Martial Laughs over Illness and Death,"* pages 123–124.

Review XII

Exercise XIIa

*Read aloud and translate. Identify each subordinate clause and tell
what type it is. Identify the tense and voice of each subjunctive and
say whether it is in primary or secondary sequence.*

1. Cornēlia tam dēfessa erat ut paene lacrimāret.
2. Cornēlius Sextum monuit nē iterum in lūdō tam ignāvus esset.
3. Iānitor eīs imperābat ut statim abīrent.
4. Matrōnae ad senātum lacrimantēs vēnērunt ut senātōribus persuādērent.
5. Servus in aquam dēsiluit nē fūr effugeret.
6. Eucleidēs puerīs persuāsit ut vēra dīcerent.
7. Cornēlia nescit cūr pater sē adesse in tablīnō iusserit.
8. Puerōs rogāvit ut extrā tablīnum manērent.
9. Gāius puerōs monet nē ē cubiculō exeant.
10. Ancillae in cubiculum festīnāvērunt ut crīnēs Aurēliae cūrārent.
11. Servus arborem ascendit nē caperētur.
12. Ille liber est tālis ut Aurēlia eum legere nōlit.
13. Tanta multitūdō ad domum convenit ut omnibus intrāre nōn liceat.
14. Tam longum erat iter ut Valerius dēfessus esset.
15. Sextum Marcus rogāvit ut sibi nārrāret quid in amphitheātrō āctum esset.
16. Prīnceps imperāvit nē servus occīderētur.
17. Cīvēs in palaestram excēdēbant ut sē exercērent.
18. Aenēās ad Hesperiam nāvigābat ut urbem novam conderet.
19. Servus casam pīrātārum celerrimē petīvit ut dominum servāret.
20. Grammaticus ferulam rapit ut Sextum verberet.
21. Praedōnēs tam celeriter cucurrērunt ut Eucleidem facile cōnsequerentur.
22. Tot et tanta erant incendia ut cīvēs aedificia servāre nōn possent.
23. Tanta tempestās coorta est ut mīlitēs nāvem cōnscendere vix possent.
24. Eucleidēs Sextō imperat nē pūpam laedat.
25. Cornēlia mātrem rogāvit ut servum arcesseret ut cum eō loquerētur.

Exercise XIIb

Read the following passage and answer the questions below in English:

At a dinner party given by Trimalchio, one of his guests, Niceros, tells the strange story of a werewolf.

Cum adhūc servus essem, in urbe Brundisiō habitābāmus. Ibi amāre coepī Melissam, mulierem pulcherrimam quae in vīllā rūsticā habitābat. Forte dominus meus Capuam discesserat. Occāsiōne datā, igitur, Melissam vīsitāre cōnstituī, sed sōlus īre nōluī. Itaque amīcō cuidam persuāsī ut mēcum ad quīntum mīliārium venīret. Ille autem erat mīles, homō audācissimus.   5
Nōs mediā nocte profectī sumus. Lūna lūcēbat tamquam merīdiē. Vēnimus inter monumenta. Homō meus coepit ad stēlās īre; sedeō ego cantābundus et stēlās numerō. Deinde, ut respexī ad comitem, ille omnia vestīmenta exūta humī prope viam posuit. Dī immortālēs! Nōlīte mē iocārī putāre! Ille subitō lupus est factus. Mihi anima in nāsō erat; stābam tamquam mortuus.   10
Postquam lupus factus est, ululāre coepit et in silvās fūgit. Ego prīmō nesciēbam ubi essem. Deinde ad stēlās prōcessī ut vestīmenta eius tollerem. Illa autem lapidea facta sunt. Paulīsper stābam immōbilis. Gladium tamen strīnxī et umbrās cecīdī, donec ad vīllam amīcae meae pervēnī. Melissa mea mīrābātur quod tam sērō ambulārem: "Sī ante vēnissēs, nōs adiuvāre potuistī.   15
Lupus enim vīllam intrāvit et omnia pecora tamquam lanius necāvit. Servus tamen noster lanceā collum eius vulnerāvit."
Haec ut audīvī, tam dēfessus eram ut statim obdormīverim. Prīmā lūce fūgī. Postquam vēnī in illum locum in quō lapidea vestīmenta erant facta, nihil invēnī nisi sanguinem. Ut domum vēnī, iacēbat mīles meus in lectō   20
tamquam bōs, et collum illīus medicus cūrābat. Intellēxī illum versipellem esse, nec posteā cum illō pānem esse potuī, nōn sī mē occīdissēs.

mīliārium, -ī (*n*), milestone	**lancea, -ae** (*f*), lance
lūna, -ae (*f*), moon	**collum, -ī** (*n*), neck
tamquam, as, just as, just like	**versipellis, versipellis** (*m*), were-
stēla, -ae (*f*), tombstone	wolf (**vertō**, to change + **pel-**
nāsus, -ī (*m*), nose	**lis**, skin)
donec, until	**esse**, to eat
vēnissēs, you had come	**occīdissēs**, you had killed
pecus, pecoris (*n*), animal, cattle	

caedō, caedere (3), **cecīdī, caesum**, to strike out at, slash at

115

1. What were Niceros' feelings for Melissa?
2. What details are we given about her?
3. Why was Niceros able to leave the house to visit her?
4. Who was to be his companion for part of the way?
5. Why did this man seem a suitable companion for the journey?
6. When did they set out?
7. How were they able to see their way in the dark?
8. Using your knowledge of Roman life and customs, indicate what stage in the journey the two men had reached when they came to the tombs.
9. What did Niceros do when they reached the tombs?
10. What strange behavior did he first observe in his companion?
11. Why had Niceros good reason to be scared?
12. What further details does he add about his companion's unnatural behavior?
13. What did Niceros now attempt to do, and why was he prevented from doing so?
14. What steps did he now take to defend himself?
15. Why do you think he "slashed at shadows" on the road?
16. Why was Melissa surprised to see him?
17. What had happened at the farm?
18. On the way home, what did Niceros find at the spot where his companion had deserted him?
19. Describe what he saw when he arrived home.
20. What conclusion did Niceros draw about his former companion, and how did he feel about him now?
21. In what way does the last sentence throw light on the derivation of the English word *companion*?
22. Find the phrase in the passage that would be equivalent to the English expression "My heart was in my mouth."

Exercise XIIc

In the passage in Exercise XIIb, locate in sequence all clauses of the following types:

1. Circumstantial **cum**.
2. Ablative absolute.
3. Indirect command.
4. Ut + indicative.
5. Indirect question.
6. Purpose.
7. Result.

VERSICULĪ

22 The Thief's Accomplice
(after Chapter 42)

"Vestīmenta malus quis mē custōde valēbit
   surripere?" Haec semper dīcere, serve, solēs.
Num nescīs furtum quam rārō fīat ab ūnō?
   Somnifer auxilium fert deus ipse suum!

valēbit, will be able
Num . . . ? Surely . . . not? (introduces a question that expects the answer
   "no"; note the implied double negative in the sentence)
furtum, -ī (*n*), theft
fīat, is committed
somnifer, somnifera, somniferum, sleep-bringing

23 A Difference of Opinion
(after Chapter 43)

Tē iuvenīlis amor, iam tē, Cornēlia, sanguis
   dēlectat causā sparsus amōris humī.
Vēmenter cum tē dissentit Sextus. "Amōris
   quis causā sānus caeditur," inquit, "homō?"

iuvenīlis, -is, -e, youthful   **causā** (+ *gen.*), for the sake of

spargō, spargere (3), **sparsī, sparsum,** to sprinkle
dissentiō, dissentīre (4), **dissēnsī, dissēnsum,** to disagree
caedō, caedere (3), **cecīdī, caesum,** to kill (*here passive in reflexive sense,*
   to kill oneself)

117

24 Sextus Reproved
(after Chapter 44)

Dīcimus haec omnēs, "Annōs tot, pessime, nātō
pūpa puellāris nūlla ferenda tibi."

annōs tot . . . nātō, so many years old
ferenda (est) tibi, ought to be carried away by you

25 Hermes the Gladiator
(after Chapter 46)

The poet Martial, whose epigrams you have already met, found much to write about
in the contests taking place in the amphitheater. In the following poem he praises
the gladiator Hermes, who excelled in no fewer than three fighting roles: as a **vēles**
lightly armed with a spear, as a **rētiārius** with net and trident, and as a **Samnīs**
heavily armed and with visored helmet. This explains why he is called **ter ūnus** in
the last line. The meter is hendecasyllabic.

Hermēs Martia saeculī voluptās,
Hermēs omnibus ērudītus armīs,
Hermēs et gladiātor et magister,
Hermēs turba suī tremorque lūdī,
Hermēs quem timet Hēlius, sed ūnum, 5
Hermēs cui cadit Advolāns, sed ūnī,
Hermēs vincere nec ferīre doctus,
Hermēs suppositīcius sibi ipse,
Hermēs dīvitiae locāriōrum,
Hermēs cūra laborque lūdiārum,   10
Hermēs belligerā superbus hastā,
Hermēs aequoreō mināx tridente,
Hermēs casside languidā timendus,
Hermēs glōria Martis ūniversī,
Hermēs omnia sōlus, et ter ūnus.   15

—Martial, *Epigrams* V.24

Hermēs: the gladiator has adopted the name of the god.

Martius, -a, -um, connected with Mars, the god of war and combat

saeculum, -ī (*n*), age, era

voluptās, voluptātis (*f*), pleasure, delight

turba, -ae (*f*), crowd, (here) confusion

suī . . . lūdī, of his school (of gladiators)

5 **Hēlius,** "Sun," and **Advolāns,** literally, "Flying to (the Attack)," were two distinguished gladiators.

sed ūnum, but the only one

feriō, ferīre (4), to strike, kill

supposītīcius sibi ipse, himself his only substitute

dīvitiae, -ārum (*f pl*), wealth, riches

locārius, -ī (*m*), a person who buys up seats (**loca**) in the amphitheater and then sells them for as high a price as he can get, a scalper

10 **cūra, -ae** (*f*), care, (here) the favorite

labor lūdiārum, the heart-throb of the female fans

belliger, belligera, belligerum, warlike (cf. the phrase **bellum gerere,** to wage war)

hasta, -ae (*f*), spear

aequoreō . . . tridente, with his sea trident (cf. **aequor, aequoris,** *n*, the sea)

mināx, minācis, menacing

cassis, cassidis (*f*), a plumed metal helmet

languidus, -a, -um, drooping (here perhaps describing the crest of the helmet drooping down over his eyes)

Martis ūniversī, of every kind of combat

15 **ter,** three times

119

26   Another Example of Caesar's Leniency (after Chapter 47)

In this epigram of Martial we find the Emperor refusing to decide the fate of two
gladiators until one or the other makes the formal sign of surrender—by raising a
hand and lowering his shield (**ad digitum levātum pōnere parmam**). He awards
them trophies (**lancēs**) in abundance as the fight proceeds, and on their simultaneous
surrender he awards to both an honorable discharge from the arena.

Cum traheret Priscus, traheret certāmina Vērus,
   esset et aequālis Mars utriusque diū,
missiō saepe virīs magnō clāmōre petīta est;
   sed Caesar lēgī pāruit ipse suae:
lēx erat ad digitum positā concurrere parmā: 5
   quod licuit, lancēs dōnaque saepe dedit.
Inventus tamen est fīnis discrīminis aequī:
   pugnāvēre parēs, succubuēre parēs.
Mīsit utrīque rudēs et palmās Caesar utrīque:
   hoc pretium virtūs ingeniōsa tulit.   10
Contigit hoc nūllō nisi tē sub prīncipe, Caesar:
   cum duo pugnārent, victor uterque fuit.

—De spectaculis XXIX

traheret . . . certāmina, was drawing out the contest
aequālis, -is, -e, equal
utriusque, *gen.* of **uterque**
missiō, missiōnis (*f*), release
lēx, lēgis (*f*), law
5 **concurrere,** (here) to fight
parma, -ae (*f*), a small, round shield
quod licuit, as the rules allowed
lanx, lancis (*f*), a metal dish, (here) a trophy
discrīmen, discrīminis (*n*), decision, test, combat
aequus, -a, -um, equal
pugnāvēre = pugnāvērunt
succumbō, succumbere (3), **succūbuī, succūbitum,** to give up, collapse
utrīque, *dat.* of **uterque**
rudis, rudis (*f*), a wooden sword given to a successful gladiator on his final
   discharge
10 **pretium, -ī,** (*n*), (here) reward
virtūs, virtūtis (*f*), courage
ingeniōsus, -a, -um, talented
contingō, contingere (3), **contigī, contactum,** to touch, (here) to happen
nisi, (here) except

27 Androcles' True Bravery
(after Chapter 48)

"Hoc volumus magnō cognōscere in Amphitheātrō—
fortis quam sit homō, bēstia quamque ferōx.
Mānsuētum nēmō māvult spectāre leōnem
lambere, quā vescī dēbuit ille, manum!"
Tālia cōniciō sentīre, ō Caesar, inānēs,   5
parcente et cēnae tē simul atque ferae;
nec meminisse queunt audācia quanta fuisset
illīus, nūllō cōnspiciente, virī;
quī laesum, gemitū resonante per antra, leōnem—
fortiter (ā!) mītis—mulsit, opemque tulit!   10

sit, present subjunctive of the verb esse, in an indirect question, "how brave a
    man is"
5 inānis, -is, -e, empty, foolish
  inānēs, -ium (m pl), foolish folk
  simul atque, at the same time as
  nec meminisse queunt, nor can they remember
  gemitus, -ūs (m), groaning
  antrum, -ī (n), cave (often used in the plural of a single cave)
10 ā!, exclamation
  mulceō, mulcēre (2), mulsī, to soothe
  ops, opis (f), help

28 Nucēs Relinquere
(middle of Chapter 50)

Nōn modo, Marce, togam, iuvenis formōse, relinquēs
praetextam, multīs testibus, ante Larēs.
Praecipit ipse pater, sēcum ut, quodcunque virīlēs
annōs nōn deceat, bulla sacrāta trahat.
"Pār!"-ne "impār!" clāmāre iuvat? Digitīsque micāre? 5
Cūnctās illa nucēs abstulit ūna diēs!

121

formōsus, -a, -um, handsome

testis, testis (*m*), witness

   multīs testibus, before many witnesses

quodcunque, whatsoever

decet, decēre (2), **decuit,** is right or fitting for, appropriate to (used with accusative)

sacrō (1), to consecrate, dedicate

trahat: (here) should take (along with it)

5 **iuvō** (1), to please, delight. (Supply **tē** as direct object.)

29 Bridal Hymn
(middle of Chapter 52)

This is part of a longer poem by Catullus. It is meant to be sung as the bride is accompanied on the evening of her wedding from her father's house to her new home. The bride's name on this occasion is Aurunculeia. In the first two stanzas she is told to dry her tears. After all, she is very beautiful! The meter is glyconic.

Flēre dēsine! Nōn tibi, Aurunculeia, perīculum est
nē qua fēmina pulchrior
clārum ab Ōceanō diem
   vīderit venientem.   5

Tālis in variō solet
dīvitis dominī hortulō
stāre flōs hyacinthinus.
Sed morāris! Abit diēs!
   Prōdeās, nova nūpta!   10

At last the chorus see the bright veil of the bride appearing. It is time for the hymn and the distribution of nuts.

Tollite, ō puerī, facēs!
Flammeum videō venīre.
Īte, concinite in modum
"Iō Hymēn Hymenaee iō,
   iō Hymēn Hymenaee!"   15

122

Da nucēs puerīs, iners
concubīne: satis diū
lūsistī nucibus. Lubet
iam servīre Talassiō.
Concubīne, nucēs da!   20

—Catullus LXI.86–95, 121–125, and 131–135

fleō, flēre (2), flēvī, flētum, to weep, cry
dēsinō, dēsinere (3), dēsiī, dēsitum, to stop
nōn . . . perīculum est nē qua, there is no danger that any
clārus, -a, -um, bright
6 varius, -a, -um, many-hued
hortulus, -ī (m), diminutive of hortus
10 prōdeō, prōdīre (irreg.), prōdiī, prōditum, to come forth. The present subjunctive prōdeās expresses a command.
fax, facis (f), wedding-torch
concinō, concinere (3), concinuī, to sing together (cf. cantō, 1, to sing)
modus, -ī (m), (here) rhythmic, harmonious manner
Iō! a ritual exclamation. (The i is consonantal, and the word is pronounced as
one syllable.)
Hymēn (m), an exclamation chanted at weddings; later thought of as the god
of weddings
Hymenaeus, -ī (m), another form of Hymēn (see above)
16 Da nucēs puerīs . . . : during the procession the bridegroom threw nuts to the
children at the side of the road.
iners, inertis, lazy
concubīnus, -ī (m), bridegroom
lubet = libet, libēre (2), libuit or libitum est, it is pleasing (to someone, dat.)
to do something (infin.). Supply tibi.
serviō (4) (+ dat.), to serve
Talassius, -ī (m), god of marriage

30 Martial Laughs over Illness and Death

(after Chapter 53)

In these epigrams, Martial sees the funny side of illness and death. The first two
poems make observations on the medical profession of 1,900 years ago.

123

(i) Symmachus Takes the Students Around

Languēbam: sed tū comitātus prōtinus ad mē
vēnistī centum, Symmache, discipulīs.
Centum mē tetigēre manūs aquilōne gelātae;
nōn habuī febrem, Symmache: nunc habeō.

—V.9

(ii) Hermocrates Who Cures All

Lōtus nōbīscum est, hilaris cēnāvit, et īdem
inventus māne est mortuus Andragorās.
Tam subitae mortis causam, Faustīne, requīris?
In somnīs medicum vīderat Hermocratem!

—VI.53

(iii) Epitaph with a Difference!

Sit tibi terra levis, mollīque tegāris harēnā
nē tua nōn possint ēruere ossa canēs!

—IX.29.11–12

langueō, languēre (2), to be ill in bed
comitātus, -a, -um, accompanied
prōtinus, immediately
tangō, tangere (3), tetigī, tactum, to touch. tetigēre = tetigērunt
aquilōne gelātae, chilled by the north wind
febris, febris (f), fever

lōtus = lavātus, one form of the perfect passive participle of lavō, to wash.
  lōtus est, he bathed
subitus, -a, -um, sudden
requīrō, requīrere (3), requīsīvī, requīsītum, to ask, inquire

sit, may (it) be
levis, -is, -e, light
mollis, -is, -e, soft
tegāris, may you be covered
harēna, -ae (f), sand
nē . . . nōn possint, so that (they) may not be unable
ēruo, ēruere (3), ēruī, ērutum, to dig up

124

FORMS

I. Nouns

Number Case	1st Declension Fem.	2nd Declension Masc.	2nd Declension Masc.	2nd Declension Neut.	3rd Declension Masc.	3rd Declension Fem.	3rd Declension Neut.	4th Declension Fem.	4th Declension Neut.	5th Declension Masc.
Singular										
Nom.	puélla	sérvus	púer	báculum	páter	vōx	nṓmen	mánus	génū	diḗs
Gen.	puéllae	sérvī	púerī	báculī	pátris	vṓcis	nṓminis	mánūs	génūs	diḗī
Dat.	puéllae	sérvō	púerō	báculō	pátrī	vṓcī	nṓminī	mánuī	génū	diḗī
Acc.	puéllam	sérvum	púerum	báculum	pátrem	vṓcem	nṓmen	mánum	génū	diem
Abl.	puéllā	sérvō	púerō	báculō	pátre	vṓce	nṓmine	mánū	génū	diḗ
Plural										
Nom.	puéllae	sérvī	púerī	bácula	pátrēs	vṓcēs	nṓmina	mánūs	génua	diḗs
Gen.	puellárum	servórum	puerórum	baculórum	pátrum	vṓcum	nṓminum	mánuum	génuum	diḗrum
Dat.	puéllīs	sérvīs	púerīs	báculīs	pátribus	vṓcibus	nōmínibus	mánibus	génibus	diḗbus
Acc.	puéllās	sérvōs	púerōs	bácula	pátrēs	vṓcēs	nṓmina	mánūs	génua	diḗs
Abl.	puéllīs	sérvīs	púerīs	báculīs	pátribus	vṓcibus	nōmínibus	mánibus	génibus	diḗbus

II. Adjectives

Number Case	1st and 2nd Declension			3rd Declension		
	Masc.	*Fem.*	*Neut.*	*Masc.*	*Fem.*	*Neut.*
Singular						
Nominative	mágnus	mágna	mágnum	ómnis	ómnis	ómne
Genitive	mágnī	mágnae	mágnī	ómnis	ómnis	ómnis
Dative	mágnō	mágnae	mágnō	ómnī	ómnī	ómnī
Accusative	mágnum	mágnam	mágnum	ómnem	ómnem	ómne
Ablative	mágnō	mágnā	mágnō	ómnī	ómnī	ómnī
Plural						
Nominative	mágnī	mágnae	mágna	ómnēs	ómnēs	ómnia
Genitive	magnórum	magnárum	magnórum	ómnium	ómnium	ómnium
Dative	mágnīs	mágnīs	mágnīs	ómnibus	ómnibus	ómnibus
Accusative	mágnōs	mágnās	mágna	ómnēs	ómnēs	ómnia
Ablative	mágnīs	mágnīs	mágnīs	ómnibus	ómnibus	ómnibus

III. Numerical Adjectives or Numbers

Case	Masc.	Fem.	Neut.	Masc.	Fem.	Neut.	Masc.	Fem.	Neut.
Nom.	ūnus	ūna	ūnum	dúo	dúae	dúo	trēs	trēs	tria
Gen.	ūníus	ūníus	ūníus	duórum	duárum	duórum	tríum	tríum	tríum
Dat.	únī	únī	únī	duóbus	duábus	duóbus	tríbus	tríbus	tríbus
Acc.	únum	únam	únum	dúōs	dúās	dúo	trēs	trēs	tria
Abl.	únō	únā	únō	duóbus	duábus	duóbus	tríbus	tríbus	tríbus

Cardinal

I	ūnus, -a, -um, one
II	duo, -ae, -o, two
III	trēs, trēs, tria, three
IV	quattuor, four
V	quīnque, five
VI	sex, six
VII	septem, seven
VIII	octō, eight
IX	novem, nine
X	decem, ten
XI	ūndecim, eleven
XII	duodecim, twelve
XX	vīgintī, twenty
L	quīnquāgintā, fifty
C	centum, a hundred
D	quīngentī, -ae, -a, five hundred
M	mīlle, a thousand

Ordinal

prīmus, -a, -um, first
secundus, -a, -um, second
tertius, -a, -um, third
quārtus, -a, -um
quīntus, -a, -um
sextus, -a, -um
septimus, -a, -um
octāvus, -a, -um
nōnus, -a, -um
decimus, -a, -um
ūndecimus, -a, -um
duodecimus, -a, -um
vīcēsimus, -a, -um
quīnquāgēsimus, -a, -um
centēsimus, -a, -um
quīngentēsimus, -a, -um
mīllēsimus, -a, -um

N.B. The cardinal numbers from **quattuor** to **centum** do not change their form to indicate case and gender.

IV. Comparative Adjectives

Number Case	Masculine	Feminine	Neuter
Singular			
Nom.	púlchrior	púlchrior	púlchrius
Gen.	pulchrióris	pulchrióris	pulchrióris
Dat.	pulchriórī	pulchriórī	pulchriórī
Acc.	pulchriórem	pulchriórem	púlchrius
Abl.	pulchrióre	pulchrióre	pulchrióre
Plural			
Nom.	pulchriórēs	pulchriórēs	pulchrióra
Gen.	pulchriórum	pulchriórum	pulchriórum
Dat.	pulchrióribus	pulchrióribus	pulchrióribus
Acc.	pulchriórēs	pulchriórēs	pulchrióra
Abl.	pulchrióribus	pulchrióribus	pulchrióribus

Adjectives have *positive, comparative,* and *superlative* forms. You can usually recognize the comparative by the letters **-ior(-)** and the superlative by **-issimus, -errimus,** or **-illimus,** e.g.:

ignāvus, *lazy*	ignāvior	ignāvissimus, -a, -um
pulcher, *beautiful*	pulchrior	pulcherrimus, -a, -um
facilis, *easy*	facilior	facillimus, -a, -um

Some adjectives are irregular in the comparative and superlative, e.g.:

bonus, *good*	melior, *better*	optimus, *best*
malus, *bad*	peior, *worse*	pessimus, *worst*
magnus, *big*	maior, *bigger*	maximus, *biggest*
parvus, *small*	minor, *smaller*	minimus, *smallest*
multus, *much*	plūs, *more*	plūrimus, *most, very much*
multī, *many*	plūrēs, *more*	plūrimī, *most, very many*

128

V. Present Active Participles

Number Case	Masculine	Feminine	Neuter
Singular			
Nom.	párāns	párāns	párāns
Gen.	parántis	parántis	parántis
Dat.	parántī	parántī	parántī
Acc.	parántem	parántem	párāns
Abl.	paránte	paránte	paránte
Plural			
Nom.	parántēs	parántēs	parántia
Gen.	parántium	parántium	parántium
Dat.	parántibus	parántibus	parántibus
Acc.	parántēs	parántēs	parántia
Abl.	parántibus	parántibus	parántibus

For all tenses and forms of participles, see Chapter 43, pages 24–5.

VI. Demonstrative Adjectives and Pronouns

Number Case	Masc.	Fem.	Neut.	Masc.	Fem.	Neut.
Singular						
Nom.	hic	haec	hoc	ílle	ílla	íllud
Gen.	húius	húius	húius	illíus	illíus	illíus
Dat.	húic	húic	húic	íllī	íllī	íllī
Acc.	hunc	hanc	hoc	íllum	íllam	íllud
Abl.	hōc	hāc	hōc	íllō	íllā	íllō
Plural						
Nom.	hī	hae	haec	íllī	íllae	ílla
Gen.	hórum	hárum	hórum	illórum	illárum	illórum
Dat.	hīs	hīs	hīs	íllīs	íllīs	íllīs
Acc.	hōs	hās	haec	íllōs	íllās	ílla
Abl.	hīs	hīs	hīs	íllīs	íllīs	íllīs

Number Case	Masc.	Fem.	Neut.	Masc.	Fem.	Neut.
Singular						
Nom.	is	éa	id	ídem	éadem	ídem
Gen.	éius	éius	éius	eiúsdem	eiúsdem	eiúsdem
Dat.	éī	éī	éī	eídem	eídem	eídem
Acc.	éum	éam	id	eúndem	eándem	ídem
Abl.	éō	éā	éō	eódem	eádem	eódem
Plural						
Nom.	éī	éae	éa	eídem	eaédem	éadem
Gen.	eórum	eárum	eórum	eōrúndem	eārúndem	eōrúndem
Dat.	éīs	éīs	éīs	eísdem	eísdem	eísdem
Acc.	éōs	éās	éa	eósdem	eásdem	éadem
Abl.	éīs	éīs	éīs	eísdem	eísdem	eísdem

VII. Indefinite Adjective

Number Case	Masc.	Fem.	Neut.
Singular			
Nom.	quídam	quaédam	quóddam
Gen.	cuiúsdam	cuiúsdam	cuiúsdam
Dat.	cúidam	cúidam	cúidam
Acc.	quéndam	quándam	quóddam
Abl.	quódam	quádam	quódam
Plural			
Nom.	quídam	quaédam	quaédam
Gen.	quōrúndam	quārúndam	quōrúndam
Dat.	quibúsdam	quibúsdam	quibúsdam
Acc.	quósdam	quásdam	quaédam
Abl.	quibúsdam	quibúsdam	quibúsdam

VIII. Intensive Adjective

Number Case	Masc.	Fem.	Neut.
Singular			
Nom.	ípse	ípsa	ípsum
Gen.	ipsíus	ipsíus	ipsíus
Dat.	ípsī	ípsī	ípsī
Acc.	ípsum	ípsam	ípsum
Abl.	ípsō	ípsā	ípsō
Plural			
Nom.	ípsī	ípsae	ípsa
Gen.	ipsórum	ipsárum	ipsórum
Dat.	ípsīs	ípsīs	ípsīs
Acc.	ípsōs	ípsās	ípsa
Abl.	ípsīs	ípsīs	ípsīs

131

IX. Adverbs

Latin adverbs may be formed from adjectives of the 1st and 2nd declensions by adding *-ē* to the base of the adjective, e.g., **strēnuē**, "strenuously," from **strēnuus, -a, -um.** To form an adverb from a 3rd declension adjective, add *-iter* to the base of the adjective or *-ter* to bases ending in -nt-, e.g., **breviter,** "briefly," from **brevis, -is, -e,** and **prūdenter,** "wisely," from **prūdēns, prūdentis.**

The comparative ends in *-ius.*
The superlative ends in *-issimē, -errimē,* or *-illimē,* e.g.:

lentē, *slowly*	lentius	lentissimē
fēlīciter, *luckily*	fēlīcius	fēlīcissimē
dīligenter, *carefully*	dīligentius	dīligentissimē
celeriter, *quickly*	celerius	celerrimē
facile, *easily*	facilius	facillimē

Some adverbs are irregular:

bene, *well*	melius, *better*	optimē, *best*
male, *badly*	peius, *worse*	pessimē, *worst*
magnopere, *greatly*	magis, *more*	maximē, *most*
paulum, *little*	minus, *less*	minimē, *least*
multum, *much*	plūs, *more*	plūrimum, *most*

Some adverbs are not formed from adjectives:

diū, *for a long time*	diūtius	diūtissimē
saepe, *often*	saepius	saepissimē
sērō, *late*	sērius	sērissimē

X. Personal and Demonstrative Pronouns

| Case | \multicolumn{6}{c}{Singular} | \multicolumn{6}{c}{Plural} |

Case	1st	2nd	3rd Masc.	3rd Fem.	3rd Neut.	1st	2nd	3rd Masc.	3rd Fem.	3rd Neut.
Nom.	égo	tū	is	éa	id	nōs	vōs	éī	éae	éa
Gen.			éius	éius	éius			eórum	eárum	eórum
Dat.	míhi	tíbi	éī	éī	éī	nóbīs	vóbīs	éīs	éīs	éīs
Acc.	mē	tē	éum	éam	id	nōs	vōs	éōs	éās	éa
Abl.	mē	tē	éō	éā	éō	nóbīs	vóbīs	éīs	éīs	éīs

132

XI. Reflexive Pronoun

	Singular	Plural
Nom.	---------	------
Gen.	súī	súī
Dat.	síbi	síbi
Acc.	sē	sē
Abl.	sē	sē

XII. Relative and Interrogative Pronouns and Adjectives

	Singular			Plural		
	Masc.	*Fem.*	*Neut.*	*Masc.*	*Fem.*	*Neut.*
Nom.	quī	quae	quod	quī	quae	quae
Gen.	cúius	cúius	cúius	quórum	quárum	quórum
Dat.	cúi	cúi	cúi	quíbus	quíbus	quíbus
Acc.	quem	quam	quod	quōs	quās	quae
Abl.	quō	quā	quō	quíbus	quíbus	quíbus

The interrogative pronoun **Quis . . . ?** has the same forms as the relative pronoun except for the nominative masculine singular **Quis . . . ?** and the nominative and accusative neuter singular **Quid . . . ?** In the singular, the feminine has the same forms as the masculine. In the plural, all forms are the same as those of the relative pronoun.

133

XIII. Regular Verbs Active: Infinitive, Imperative, Indicative

				1st Conjugation	2nd Conjugation	3rd Conjugation		4th Conjugation
Present Infinitive				paráre	habére	míttere	iácere (-iö)	audíre
Imperative	Singular		2	párá	hábé	mítte	iáce	aúdí
			3	paráte	habéte	míttite	iácite	audíte
	Plural							
Present	Singular		1	párö	hábeö	míttö	iáciö	aúdiö
			2	párás	hábés	míttis	iácis	aúdís
			3	párat	hábet	míttit	iácit	aúdit
	Plural		1	parámus	habémus	míttimus	iácimus	audímus
			2	parátis	habétis	míttitis	iácitis	audítis
			3	párant	hábent	míttunt	iáciunt	aúdiunt
Imperfect	Singular		1	parábam	habébam	mittébam	iaciébam	audiébam
			2	parábás	habébás	mittébás	iaciébás	audiébás
			3	parábat	habébat	mittébat	iaciébat	audiébat
	Plural		1	parábámus	habébámus	mittébámus	iaciébámus	audiébámus
			2	parábátis	habébátis	mittébátis	iaciébátis	audiébátis
			3	parábant	habébant	mittébant	iaciébant	audiébant

XIII. Regular Verbs Active: Indicative, Infinitive (continued)

		parābō	habēbō	mittam	iaciam	audiam
Future	Singular 1	parábō	habḗbō	míttam	iáciam	aúdiam
	2	parábis	habḗbis	míttēs	iáciēs	aúdiēs
	3	parábit	habḗbit	míttet	iáciet	aúdiet
	Plural 1	parábimus	habḗbimus	mittḗmus	iaciḗmus	audiḗmus
	2	parábitis	habḗbitis	mittḗtis	iaciḗtis	audiḗtis
	3	parábunt	habḗbunt	míttent	iácient	aúdient
Perfect Infinitive		parāvísse	habuísse	mīsísse	iēcísse	audīvísse
Perfect	Singular 1	parā́vī	hábuī	mī́sī	iḗcī	audī́vī
	2	parāvístī	habuístī	mīsístī	iēcístī	audīvístī
	3	parā́vit	hábuit	mī́sit	iḗcit	audī́vit
	Plural 1	parā́vimus	habúimus	mī́simus	iḗcimus	audī́vimus
	2	parāvístis	habuístis	mīsístis	iēcístis	audīvístis
	3	parāvḗrunt	habuḗrunt	mīsḗrunt	iēcḗrunt	audīvḗrunt

135

XIII. Regular Verbs Active: Indicative (continued)

			paráre	habére	míttere	iácere	audíre
Pluperfect	*Singular*	1	paráveram	habúeram	míseram	iéceram	audíveram
		2	paráverás	habúerás	míserás	iécerás	audíverás
		3	paráverat	habúerat	míserat	iécerat	audíverat
	Plural	1	paráverámus	habuerámus	míserámus	iécerámus	audíverámus
		2	paráverátis	habuerátis	míserátis	iécerátis	audiverátis
		3	paráverant	habúerant	míserant	iécerant	audíverant
Future Perfect	*Singular*	1	paráverō	habúerō	míserō	iécerō	audíverō
		2	paráveris	habúeris	míseris	iéceris	audíveris
		3	paráverit	habúerit	míserit	iécerit	audíverit
	Plural	1	paráverimus	habuérimus	misérimus	iécérimus	audivérimus
		2	paráveritis	habuéritis	miséritis	iécéritis	audivéritis
		3	paráverint	habúerint	míserint	iécerint	audíverint

136

XIV. Regular Verbs Passive: Indicative

			1st Conjugation	2nd Conjugation	3rd Conjugation		4th Conjugation
Present	Singular	1	pórtor	móveor	míttor	iácior	aúdior
		2	portáris	movéris	mítteris	iáceris	audíris
		3	portátur	movétur	míttitur	iácitur	audítur
	Plural	1	portámur	movémur	míttimur	iácimur	audímur
		2	portáminī	movéminī	mittíminī	iacíminī	audíminī
		3	portántur	movéntur	mittúntur	iaciúntur	audiúntur
Imperfect	Singular	1	portábar	movébar	mittébar	iaciébar	audiébar
		2	portābáris	movēbáris	mittēbáris	iaciēbáris	audiēbáris
		3	portābátur	movēbátur	mittēbátur	iaciēbátur	audiēbátur
	Plural	1	portābámur	movēbámur	mittēbámur	iaciēbámur	audiēbámur
		2	portābáminī	movēbáminī	mittēbáminī	iaciēbáminī	audiēbáminī
		3	portābántur	movēbántur	mittēbántur	iaciēbántur	audiēbántur

137

XIV. Regular Verbs Passive: Indicative (continued)

Future	Singular	1	portábor	movébor	míttar	iáciar	aúdiar
		2	portáberis	movéberis	mittéris	iaciéris	audiéris
		3	portábitur	movébitur	mittétur	iaciétur	audiétur
	Plural	1	portábimur	movébimur	mittémur	iaciémur	audiémur
		2	portábiminī	movébiminī	mittéminī	iaciéminī	audiéminī
		3	portábúntur	movébúntur	mīténtur	iaciéntur	audiéntur

		PERFECT PASSIVE		PLUPERFECT PASSIVE		FUTURE PERFECT PASSIVE	
Singular	1	portátus, -a	sum	portátus, -a	éram	portátus, -a	érō
	2	portátus, -a	es	portátus, -a	érās	portátus, -a	éris
	3	portátus, -a, -um	est	portátus, -a, -um	érat	portátus, -a, -um	érit
Plural	1	portátī, -ae	súmus	portátī, -ae	erámus	portátī, -ae	érimus
	2	portátī, -ae	éstis	portátī, -ae	erátis	portátī, -ae	éritis
	3	portátī, -ae, -a	sunt	portátī, -ae, -a	érant	portátī, -ae, -a	érunt

XV. Irregular Verbs: Infinitive, Imperative, Indicative

Infinitive			ésse	pósse	vélle	nólle
Imperative			es éste	— —	— —	nólī nōlíte
Present	*Singular*	1 2 3	sum es est	póssum pótes pótest	vólō vīs vult	nólō nōn vīs nōn vult
	Plural	1 2 3	súmus éstis sunt	póssumus potéstis póssunt	vólumus vúltis vólunt	nólumus nōn vúltis nólunt
Imperfect	*Singular*	1 2 3	éram érās érat	póteram póterās póterat	volébam volébās volébat	nōlébam nōlébās nōlébat
	Plural	1 2 3	erámus erátis érant	poterámus poterátis póterant	volēbámus volēbátis volébant	nōlēbámus nōlēbátis nōlébant
Future	*Singular*	1 2 3	érō éris érit	póterō póteris póterit	vólam vólēs vólet	nólam nólēs nólet
	Plural	1 2 3	érimus éritis érunt	potérimus potéritis póterunt	volémus volétis vólent	nōlémus nōlétis nólent

XV: Irregular Verbs: Infinitive, Imperative, Indicative (continued)

Infinitive			málle	íre	férre	férrī	fíerī
Imperative			—	í	fer	férre	—
			—	íte	férte	fermínī	—
Present	Singular	1	málō	éō	férō	féror	fíō
		2	mávīs	īs	fers	férris	fīs
		3	mávult	it	fert	fértur	fit
	Plural	1	málumus	ímus	férimus	férimur	fímus
		2	mávúltis	ítis	fértis	fermínī	fítis
		3	málunt	éunt	férunt	ferúntur	fíunt
Imperfect	Singular	1	málébam	íbam	ferébam	ferébar	fiébam
		2	málébās	íbās	ferébās	ferébáris	fiébās
		3	málébat	íbat	ferébat	ferébátur	fiébat
	Plural	1	málēbámus	ībámus	ferēbámus	ferēbámur	fiēbámus
		2	málēbátis	ībátis	ferēbátis	ferēbáminī	fiēbátis
		3	málébant	íbant	ferébant	ferēbántur	fiébant
Future	Singular	1	málam	íbō	féram	férar	fíam
		2	málēs	íbis	férēs	feréris	fíēs
		3	málet	íbit	féret	ferétur	fíet
	Plural	1	málémus	íbimus	ferémus	ferémur	fiémus
		2	málétis	íbitis	ferétis	ferémínī	fiétis
		3	málent	íbunt	férent	feréntur	fíent

Note: perfect, pluperfect, and future perfect tenses are formed regularly from the perfect stem plus the regular endings for each tense. These tenses of fíō are made up of the participle **factus, -a, -um** plus **sum, eram,** and **erō** respectively.

XVI. Subjunctive

For the present subjunctive of all verbs, see Chapter 49, pages 75–76.

For the imperfect subjunctive of all verbs, see Chapter 41, pages 10–11.

For the perfect subjunctive of all verbs, see Chapter 49, page 76.

For the pluperfect subjunctive of all verbs, see Chapter 41, page 11.

XVII. Infinitives

For all tenses and forms of the infinitive, see Chapter 46, page 56.

XVIII. Participles

For all tenses and forms of the participle, see Chapter 43, pages 24–5.

Vocabulary

A

ā, ab (+ *abl.*), by, from, away from

ábeō, -íre (*irreg.*), **-ii, -itum,** to go away

abhínc (+ *acc.*), ago, previously

abrípiō, -ípere (3), **-ípuī, -éptum,** to snatch away

ábsum, abésse (*irreg.*), **áfuī,** to be away, be distant from

ac, and

áccidit, -ere (3), **-it,** to happen

accípiō, -ípere (3), **-épī, -éptum,** to receive, get, welcome

accúmbō, -mbere (3), **-buī, -bitum,** to recline (at table)

46 **ácriter,** fiercely

ad (+ *acc.*), to, towards, at, near

49 **ádeō,** so much, to such an extent

ádeō, -íre (*irreg.*), **-iī, -itum,** to come to, approach

adhúc, still, as yet

ádimō, -ímere (3), **-émī, -émptum** (+ *dat.*), to take away (from)

ádiuvō, -iuváre (1), **-iúvī, -iútum,** to help

46 **admīrátiō, -ónis** (*f*), amazement

46 **admīrātióne cáptus,** in utter amazement

47 **admīrātiónī ésse,** to be a source of wonder or surprise (to)

47 **admíror, -árī** (1), **-átus sum,** to wonder (at)

41 **admíttō, -íttere** (3), **-ísī, -íssum,** to commit (a crime)

adstántēs, -ntium (*m pl*), bystanders

ádstō, -áre (1), **-itī,** to stand near, stand by

ádsum, -ésse (*irreg.*), **-fuī,** to be present, near

aduléscēns, -ntis (*m*), young man, youth

advéniō, -veníre (4), **-vénī, -véntum,** to come to, reach, arrive at

advesperáscit, -áscere (3), **-ávit,** it is getting dark

aedifícium, -ī (*n*), building

aedíficō (1), to build

aéger, aégra, aégrum, ill

aegrótō (1), to be ill

afféctus, -a, -um, affected, moved, overcome

áfferō, -rre (*irreg.*), **áttulī, allátum,** to bring, bring to, bring in

Áge! Ágite! Come! Come on!

áger, ágrī (*m*), field, territory, land

ágō, ágere (3), **égī, áctum,** to do, drive, discuss, debate

50 **grátiās ágere** (+ *dat.*), to thank

Quid ágis? How are you?

49 **áit,** (he, she) says, said

52 **álbus, -a, -um,** white

46 **áliās,** at another time

áliquī, áliqua, áliquod, some (or other)

áliquis, áliquid, someone, something

44 **áliquid málī,** some harm

51 **nē quis** (**quis** = **áliquis**), that no one

50 **sī quis** (**quis** = **áliquis**), if anyone

álius, ália, áliud, other, another, different, one . . . another

áliī . . . áliī . . . , some . . . others . . .

álter, áltera, álterum, the one, the other (of two), the second

44 **ámbō, ámbae, ámbō**, both
ámbulō (1), to walk
amíca, -ae (f), friend
amícus, -ī (m), friend
ámō (1), to like, love
ámor, -óris (m), love
amphitheátrum, -ī (n), amphitheater
50 **ampléctor, -ctī** (3), -xus sum, to embrace
51 **an**, or
51 **útrum . . . an . . . ,** whether . . . or . . .
ancílla, -ae (f), slave-woman
ánimus, -ī (m), mind, spirit, will
ánimum recuperáre, to regain one's senses
in ánimō habére, to intend
44 **Bónō ánimō es (éste)! Cheer up!**
ánnus, -ī (m), year
ánte (+ acc.), before, in front of
ánte (adverb), before
ánteā, previously, before
ántequam, before
49 **ánulus, -ī** (m), ring
apériō, -íre (4), -uī, -tum, to open
41 **apodytérium, -ī** (n), changing-room
46 **appáritor, -óris** (m), gate-keeper, public servant
appropínquō (1) (+ dat.), to approach, draw near to
49 **áptō** (1), to place, fit
ápud (+ acc.), at the house of
áqua, -ae (f), water
52 **ára, -ae** (f), altar
árbor, -oris (f), tree
arcéssō, -ere (3), -ívī, -ítum, to summon, send for
52 **árdeō, -dére** (2), -sī, to burn, blaze
aréna, -ae (f), arena, sand
ascéndō, -dere (3), -dī, -sum, to climb
43 **aspérgō, -gere** (3), -sī, -sum, to sprinkle, splash, spatter
at, but

átque, and, also
átrium, -ī (n), atrium, main room
atténtē, attentively, closely
attónitus, -a, -um, astonished, astounded
aúdāx, -ácis, bold
aúdiō (4), to hear, listen to
aúferō, -rre (irreg.), **ábstulī, ablátum**, to carry away, take away
aufúgiō, -fúgere (3), -fúgī, to run away, escape
aúreus, -a, -um, golden
52 **aúspex, -icis** (m), augur, officiating priest
aut, or
aut . . . aut . . . , either . . . or . . .
aútem, however, but, moreover
auxílium, -ī (n), help
Ávē! Avéte! Hail! Greetings!
53 **āvértō, -tere** (3), -tī, -sum, to turn away, divert
49 **ávis, -is** (m/f), bird

B

báculum, -ī (n), stick
41 **bálneae, -árum** (f pl), baths
béne, well
50 **benevoléntia, -ae** (f), kindness
48 **béstia, -ae** (f), beast
47 **bēstiárius, -a, -um**, involving wild beasts
bíbō, -ere (3), -ī, to drink
47 **blándē**, in a friendly way
bónus, -a, -um, good
44 **Bónō ánimō es (éste)! Cheer up!**
bōs, bóvis (m/f), ox, cow
brévis, -is, -e, short
brévī témpore, in a short time
Británnī, -órum (m pl), Britons
Británnia, -ae (f), Britain
50 **búlla, -ae** (f), luck-charm, locket

C

cádō, -ere (3), cécidī, cásum, to fall

caélum, -ī (n), the sky, heaven

41 caldárium, -ī (n), hot room (at baths)

41 calor, -óris (m), heat

41 cálvus, -a, -um, bald

41 cámpus, -ī (m), plain, field

41 Cámpus Mártius, the Plain of Mars on the outskirts of Rome

53 candéla, -ae (f), candle

cántō (1), to sing

41 capillátus, -a, -um, with long hair

53 capíllī, -órum (m pl), hair

53 capíllīs solútīs, with dishevelled hair

cápiō, -ere (3), cépī, -tum, to take, capture

43 cōnsílium cápere, to adopt a plan

cáput, -itis (n), head

52 cárus, -a, -um, dear, beloved

cása, -ae (f), hut

51 catérva, -ae (f), crowd

caúda, -ae (f), tail

caúpō, -ónis (m), innkeeper

caúsa, -ae (f), cause, reason

51 genitive + causā, for the sake of, as

48 cávea, -ae (f), cage

cáveō, -ére (2), cávī, caútum, to watch out, be careful

celéritās, -átis (f), speed

súmmā celeritáte, with the greatest speed, as fast as possible

celériter, quickly

quam celérrimē, as quickly as possible

célō (1), to hide, conceal

céna, -ae (f), dinner

cénō (1), to dine, eat dinner

cértus, -a, -um, certain

cértē, certainly, at least

45 prō cértō hábeō, I am sure

céterī, -ae, -a, the rest, the others, other

cíbus, -ī (m), food

círcum (+ acc.), around

46 circumspíciō, -ícere (3), -éxī, -éctum, to look around

Círcus, -ī (m), Circus Maximus

císta, -ae (f), trunk, chest

cívis, -is (m), citizen

clámō (1), to shout

clámor, -óris (m), shout, shouting

claúdō, -dere (3), -sī, -sum, to shut, close

47 claúdus, -a, -um, lame

47 cleménter, quietly, gently

clíēns, -ntis (m), client, dependent

coépī, I began

cógitō (1), to think, consider

51 cognómen, -inis (n), nickname

41 cognóscō, -óscere (3), -óvī, -itum, to find out, learn, hear of

47 cógō, -ere (3), coégī, coáctum, to compel, force

cólloquor, -quī (3), -cútus sum, to speak together, converse

cómes, -itis (m/f), companion

50 comitor, -árī (1), -átus sum, to accompany

53 commémorō (1), to mention, comment on, recount

commissátiō, -ónis (f), drinking party

46 committō, -íttere (3), -ísī, -íssum, to bring together, entrust

46 púgnam commíttere, to join battle

53 cómmodus, -a, -um, pleasant

commótus, -a, -um, moved, excited

írā commótus, in a rage, made angry

43 commúnis, -is, -e, common

cómpleō, -ére (2), -évī, -étum, to fill, complete

complúrēs, -ēs, -a, several

52 compónō, -ónere (3), -ósuī, -ósitum, to compose

144

41 cóncrepō, -áre (1), -uī, to snap (the fingers)

concúrrō, -rere (3), -rī, -sum, to run together, rush up

concúrsō (1), to run to and fro, run about

47 condémnō (1), to condemn

cóndō, -ere (3), -idī, -itum, to found, establish

53 (mérita) cónferō, -rre (irreg.), cóntulī, collátum, to render (services to)

confíciō, -ícere (3), -ēcī, -éctum, to accomplish, finish

42 cōnfúgiō, -úgere (3), -úgī, to flee for refuge

45 congrédior, -dī (3), -ssus sum, to come together

coníciō, -ícere (3), -iēcī, -iéctum, to throw, guess

cónor, -árī (1), -átus sum, to try

50 cónsecrō (1), to dedicate

47 cōnsénsus, -ūs (m), agreement

cónsequor, -quī (3), -cútus sum, to follow, catch up to, overtake

cōnsídō, -sídere (3), -sédī, to sit down

43 cōnsílium, -ī (n), plan

43 cōnsílium cápere, to adopt a plan

46 cōnsístō, -sístere (3), -stitī, to halt, stop, stand

cōnspíciō, -ícere (3), -éxī, -éctum, to catch sight of

45 cónstat, it is agreed

cōnstítuō, -úere (3), -uī, -útum, to decide

51 cōnsúltum, -ī (n), decree

50 conticéscō, -éscere (3), -uī, to become silent

contíneō, -inére (2), -ínuī, -éntum, to confine, hold

46 cóntrā (+ acc.), opposite, in front of, facing

convaléscō, -éscere (3), -uī, to grow stronger, get well

convéniō, -eníre (4), -énī, -éntum, to come together, meet, assemble

49 convérsus, -a, -um, having turned, turning

46 convértō, -tere (3), -tī, -sum, to turn (around)

convíva, -ae (m), guest (at a banquet)

coórior, -írī (4), -tus sum, to rise up, arise

cóquus, -ī (m), cook

53 cor, córdis (n), heart

46 córnicen, -inis (m), horn-player, bugler

coróna, -ae (f), garland, crown

córpus, -oris (n), body

cotídiē, daily, every day

53 cóxa, -ae (f), hipbone

crās, tomorrow

crédō, -ere (3), -idī, -itum (+ dat.), to trust, believe

creō (1), to appoint, create

crínis, -is (m), hair

crūdélis, -is, -e, cruel

crūdélitās, -átis (f), cruelty

cubículum, -ī (n), bedroom

culína, -ae (f), kitchen

cum (+ abl.), with

cum, when, since, whenever

cum prímum, as soon as

cúnctī, -ae, -a, all

cúpiō, -ere (3), -ívī, -ítum, to desire, want

Cūr . . . ? Why . . . ?

cúra, -ae (f), care, anxiety

49 cúrae ésse, to be a cause of anxiety (to)

Cúria, -ae (f), Senate House

cúrō (1), to look after, take care of

cúrrō, -rere (3), cucúrrī, -sum, to run

custódiō (4), to guard

cústōs, -ódis (m), guard

D

dē (+ *abl.*), down from, concerning, about

52 **dēcédō**, **-dere** (3), **-ssī**, **-ssum**, to die

49 **décet** (+ *acc.*), (someone) should

49 **déditus**, **-a**, **-um**, devoted, dedicated

49 **dēdúcō**, **-cere** (3), **-xī**, **-ctum**, to show into, bring, escort

dēféssus, **-a**, **-um**, weary, tired

41 **défricō**, **-áre** (1), **-uī**, **-tum**, to rub down

deínde, then

dēléctō (1), to delight

déleō, **-ére** (2), **-évī**, **-étum**, to destroy

46 **dēlíciae**, **-árum** (*f pl*), delight

49 **dēmíssus**, **-a**, **-um**, downcast, lowered

49 **vúltū dēmíssō**, with eyes lowered

dēmíttō, **-íttere** (3), **-ísī**, **-íssum**, to let down, suspend

depṓnō, **-ónere** (3), **-ósuī**, **-ósitum**, to lay down, put aside, set down

dēscéndō, **-dere** (3), **-dī**, **-sum**, to climb down, go down

dēsíderō (1), to long for, desire, miss

dēsíliō, **-íre** (4), **-uī**, to leap down

49 **dēspóndeō**, **-dére** (2), **-dī**, **-sum**, to betroth, promise in marriage

déus, **déī** (*m*), (*dat.* and *abl. pl.* **dīs**), god

Dī immortálēs! Immortal gods! Good heavens!

Prō dī immortálēs! Good heavens!

dī mánēs, the spirits of the dead

dévorō (1), to devour

52 **déxtra**, **-ae** (*f*), right hand

dícō, **-cere** (3), **-xī**, **-ctum**, to say, tell

díēs, **-éī** (*m*), day

in díēs, every day, day by day

44 **diēs nātális**, birthday

41 **dígitus**, **-ī** (*m*), finger

44 **dígitīs micáre**, to play morra

dīligénter, carefully

53 **díligō**, **-ígere** (3), **-éxī**, **-éctum**, to love, have special regard for

50 **dīmíttō**, **-íttere** (3), **-ísī**, **-íssum**, to send away, let go

discédō, **-dere** (3), **-ssī**, **-ssum**, to depart, leave, go away

discrímen, **-inis** (*n*), distinction

díū, for a long time

díves, **-itis**, rich

dō, **dáre** (1), **dédī**, **dátum**, to give

44 **dṓnō dáre**, to give as a gift

dóceō, **-ére** (2), **-uī**, **-tum**, to teach

dóleō (2), to be sorry, be sad, to hurt

dolor, **-óris** (*m*), grief, pain

dóminus, **-ī** (*m*), master, owner

dómus, **-ūs** (*f*), house, home

dómī, at home

dómō, from home

dómum, (to) home, to the home

44 **dṓnum**, **-ī** (*n*), gift

44 **dṓnō dáre**, to give as a gift

dórmiō (4), to sleep

dúbium, **-ī** (*n*), doubt

dúcō, **-cere** (3), **-xī**, **-ctum**, to lead, take

52 **exséquiās dúcere**, to carry out the funeral rites

dum, while, as long as

dúo, **dúae**, **dúo**, two

E

ē, **ex** (+ *abl.*), from, out of, of

ébrius, **-a**, **-um**, drunk

Écce! Look at . . . ! Look!

édō, **ésse** (*irreg.*), **édī**, **ésum**, to eat

ēdúcō, **-cere** (3), **-xī**, **-ctum**, to lead out

éfferō, **-rre** (*irreg.*), **éxtulī**, **ēlátum**, to bring out, carry out (for burial)

146

effúgiō, -úgere (3), -úgī, to escape
égo, I
ēgrédior, -edī (3), -éssus sum, to go
   out, leave, disembark
Éheu! Alas!
élegāns, -ntis, elegant, tasteful
émo, émere (3), émī, émptum, to
   buy
énim (postpositive), for
51 ēnúntiō (1), to reveal, divulge
éō, íre (irreg.), ívī, ítum, to go
éō (adverb), there, to that place
51 éō mágis, all the more
epístula, -ae (f), letter
49 épulae, -árum (f pl), banquet, feast
50 érgā (+ acc.), towards
ērudítus, -a, -um, learned, schol-
   arly
ēsúriō (4), to be hungry
et, and, also
   et . . . et, both . . . and
étiam, also, even
Eúge! Hurray!
ēvádō, -dere (3), -sī, -sum, to
   escape
ex, ē (+ abl.), from, out of
47 exanimátus (métū), paralyzed (with
   fear)
53 excédō, -dere (3), -ssī, -ssum, to go
   out, leave
53 ē vítā excédere, to die
éxcitō (1), to stir up, excite, rouse,
   wake up
exclámō (1), to shout out
éxeō, -íre (irreg.), -íī, -itum, to go
   out
41 exérceō (2), to exercise, train
57 exímius, -a, -um, outstanding
53 éximō, -ímere (3), -émī, -émptum,
   to remove
expérior, -írī (4), -tus sum, to test,
   try
43 éxprimō, -ímere (3), -éssī, -éssum,
   to press out, express
52 exséquiae, -árum (f pl), funeral rites

52 exséquiās dúcere, to carry out the
   funeral rites
42 exsíliō, -íre (4), -uī, to leap out
exspéctō (1), to look out for, wait
   for
53 éxstruō, -ere (3), -xī, -ctum, to
   build
éxtrā (+ acc.), outside
éxtrahō, -here (3), -xī, -ctum, to
   pull out, drag out
41 éxuō, -úere (3), -uī, -útum, to take
   off

F
fábula, -ae (f), story
fácile, easily
fáciō, -ere (3), fécī, fáctum, to
   make, do
50 família, -ae (f), family, household
53 familiárēs, -ium (m pl), close friends
50 familiáris, -is, -e, (belonging to the)
   family or household
53 fáscēs, -ium (m pl), rods (symbol of
   office)
53 fébris, -is (f), fever
52 Fēlíciter! Good luck!
félīx, -ícis, happy, lucky, fortunate
46 fémina, -ae (f), woman
44 férē, almost, approximately
fēriátus, -a, -um, celebrating a holi-
   day
férō, -rre (irreg.), túlī, látum, to
   carry, bring, bear
feróciter, fiercely
férōx, -ócis, fierce
férula, -ae (f), cane
festínō (1), to hurry
51 fídēs, -eī (f), good faith, reliability,
   trust
fília, -ae (f), daughter
fílius, -ī (m), son
fíō, fíerī (irreg.), fáctus sum, to
   become, be made, be done,
   happen

52 **flámmeum, -ī** (*n*), orange (bridal) veil
41 **fóllis, -is** (*m*), bag
fortásse, perhaps
43 **fórte** (*adverb*), by chance
fórtis, -is, -e, brave
fortūnátus, -a, -um, happy, lucky
Fórum, -ī (*n*), Forum, market place
53 **frángō, -ngere** (3), **frḗgī, -ctum**, to break
fráter, -tris (*m*), brother
frīgidárium, -ī (*n*), cold room (at baths)
frígidus, -a, -um, cold
frū́strā, in vain
fúgiō, -ere (3), **fū́gī**, to flee
53 **fū́nebris, -is, -e**, funeral
52 **fū́nus, -eris** (*n*), funeral
42 **fūr, -ris** (*m*), thief
46 **fúror, -óris** (*m*), frenzy
fúrtim, stealthily

G

Gállī, -órum (*m pl*), Gauls
Gállia, -ae (*f*), Gaul
gaúdeō, -dḗre (2), **gāvī́sus sum**, to rejoice
gémō, -ere (3), **-uī, -itum**, to groan
49 **gēns, -tis** (*f*), family, clan
46 **génus, -eris** (*n*), kind, race
gérō, -rere (3), **-ssī, -stum**, to wear, carry on
46 **gladiátor, -óris** (*m*), gladiator
gládius, -ī (*m*), sword
53 **gnátus (nátus), -ī** (*m*), son
grammáticus, -ī (*m*), teacher
50 **grátiās ágere** (+ *dat.*), to thank
49 **grátulor, -árī** (1), **-átus sum** (+ *dat.*), to congratulate
53 **grátus, -a, -um**, pleasing, dear (to), loved (by)
grávis, -is, -e, heavy, serious

H

hábeō (2), to have, hold
45 **prō cértō hábeō**, I am sure
hábitō (1), to live, dwell
haéreō, -rḗre (2), **-sī, -sum**, to stick, cling
41 **harpástum, -ī** (*n*), ball game, hand ball
41 **haud**, not
héri, yesterday
Heu! = Éheu!
49 **Heús! Ho there!**
hic, haec, hoc, this
hīc (*adverb*), here
53 **hílaris, -is, -e**, cheerful
52 **hiláritās, -átis** (*f*), good humor, merriment
hódiē, today
hómō, -inis (*m*), man, fellow
hóminēs, -inum (*m pl*), people
51 **honóris caúsā**, as an honor
hóra, -ae (*f*), hour
50 **hórtor, -árī** (1), **-átus sum**, to encourage, urge
hóspes, -itis (*m*), friend, guest
hūc, here, to here
hūc illū́c, here and there, this way and that
46 **hūmánus, -a, -um**, human
43 **húmī**, on the ground

I

iáceō (2), to lie, be lying down
iáciō, -ere (3), **iḗcī, -ctum**, to throw
iam, now, already
iánitor, -óris (*m*), doorkeeper
iánua, -ae (*f*), door
íbi, there
id quod, (a thing) which
ídem, éadem, ídem, the same
ígitur, therefore
ignávus, -a, -um, cowardly, lazy

ignóro (1), to be ignorant, not to know

ílle, ílla, íllud, that, he, she, it

illúc, there, to that place   51
húc illúc, here and there, this way and that

imágō, -inis (f), likeness, mask   53

immánis, -is, -e, huge

immíttō, -íttere (3), -ísī, -íssum, to send in, hurl at, hurl into, let loose, release   53

immóbilis, -is, -e, motionless

immortális, -is, -e, immortal   43

Dī immortálēs! Immortal gods!   50
Good heavens!

Prō dī immortálēs! Good heavens!   48

ímpar (see pār)

ímperō (1) (+ dat.), to order   50

ímpetus, -ūs (m), attack   48

impónō, -ónere (3), -ósuī, -ósitum, to place on, put   3
in (+ abl.), in, on, among

in (+ acc.), into, towards, until   52
in díēs, every day, day by day   47

incédō, -dere (3), -ssī, to march, go   6   51

incéndium, -ī (n), fire

incéndō, -dere (3), -dī, -sum, to burn, set on fire

incéssus, -ūs (m), bearing, walk(ing)   3

íncidō, -ere (3), -ī, incásum, to fall into (on to)   3

incípiō, -ípere (3), -épī, -éptum, to begin   8

íncitō (1), to spur on, urge on, rouse

íncola, -ae (m/f), inhabitant, tenant

incúrrō, -rere (3), -rī, -sum, to run into

índe, from there, then

índuō, -úere (3), -uī, -útum, to put on

íneō, -íre (irreg.), -iī, -itum, to go in

Ínferī, -órum (m pl), the underworld, gods of the underworld

īnfírmus, -a, -um, weak, shaky, frail

ingénium, -ī (n), intelligence, ingenuity

íngēns, -ntis, huge, big

ingravéscō, -ere (3), to grow worse

ingrédior, -dī (3), -ssus sum, to go in, enter

iníciō, -ícere (3), -iécī, -iéctum, to throw into, thrust

ínquit, he (she) says, said

īnscius, -a, -um, not knowing

īnscríbō, -bere (3), -psī, -ptum, to write in, register

ínsula, -ae (f), island, tenement

intéllegō,-gere (3), -xī, -ctum, to understand, realize

ínter (+ acc.), between, among

intéreā, meanwhile

interpéllō (1), to interrupt

intérrogō (1), to ask

íntrō (1), to enter

introdúcō, -cere (3), -xī, -ctum, to bring in

intróeō, -íre (irreg.), -iī, -itum, to enter

invéniō, -eníre (4), -énī, -éntum, to come upon, find

invítō (1), to invite

invítus, -a, -um, unwilling

iócor, -árī (1), -átus sum, to joke

iócus, -ī (m), joke, funny story

ípse, ípsa, ípsum, -self

íra, -ae (f), anger

īrā commótus, made angry, in a rage

īrācúndus, -a, -um, irritable, in a bad mood

īrátus, -a, -um, angry

irrúmpō, -úmpere (3), -úpī, -úptum, to burst in, attack

is, ea, id, he, she, it, this, that

id quod, (a thing) which

íta, thus, in this way
Íta vérō! Yes!
ítaque, and so, therefore
íter, itíneris (n), journey, road
íterum, again, a second time
iúbeō, -bére (2), -ssī, -ssum, to
   order
53 iucúndus, -a, -um, pleasant, a
   delight
45 Iudaéus, -ī (m), Jew
46 iúgulō (1), to kill, murder
Iúlius, -ī (m), July
52 iúngō, -gere (3), -xī, -ctum, to join
49 iúvenis, -is (m), young man

L

42 lábor, -bī (3), -psus sum, to slip,
   stumble
labórō (1), to work
43 lácrima, -ae (f), tear
lácrimō (1), to weep, cry
44 laédō, -dere (3), -sī, -sum, to harm
laétus, -a, -um, joyful, happy
laétē, joyfully
47 lámbō, -ere (3), -ī, to lick
lána, -ae (f), wool
lánius, -ī (m), butcher
46 lanísta, -ae (m), trainer
lapídeus, -a, -um, of stone, stony
50 larárium, -ī (n), shrine of household
   gods
50 Lárēs, -um (m pl), household gods
47 látεō (2), to lie in hiding, hide
44 latrúnculus, -ī (m), robber, (pl)
   pawns (a game like chess)
44   lúdus latrunculórum, game of
   bandits
laúdō (1), to praise
52 laúrus, -ī (f), bay (tree), laurel
lávō, -áre (1), lávī, -átum or lótum,
   to wash
lectíca, -ae (f), litter
léctus, -ī (m), bed, couch
légō, -ere (3), légī, léctum, to read

léntē, slowly
43 léō, -ốnis (m), lion
53 lépidus, -a, -um, charming
53 lévis, -is, -e, smooth
libénter, gladly
líber, -brī (m), book
50 Līberália, -ium (n pl), the Liberalia
   (Festival of Liber)
líberī, -ốrum (n pl), children
47 líberō (1), to set free
53 lībérta, -ae (f), freedwoman
lībértus, -ī (m), freedman
lícet, -ére (2), -uit (+ dat.), it is
   allowed
53 líctor, -ốris (m), lictor, officer
50 límen, -inis (n), threshold, doorway
língua, -ae (f), tongue, language
53 línquō, -ere (3), líquī, to leave
41 línteum, -ī (n), towel
53 lócō (1), to place
lócus, -ī (m; n in pl), place
lóngus, -a, -um, long
lóngē, far
lóquor, -ī (3), locútus sum, to
   speak, talk
53 lúbricus, -a, -um, slippery
53 lucérna, -ae (f), lamp
lúcet, -ére (2), lúxit, to be light, to
   shine
41 lúctor, -árī (1), -átus sum, to wrestle
lúdō, -dere (3), -sī, -sum, to play
lúdus, -ī (m), game, school
lúdī, -ốrum (m pl), games (as in
   the Circus)
lúpus, -ī (m), wolf
lūx, lúcis (f), light
príma lūx, dawn

M

mágis, more
51 éō mágis, all the more
magíster, -trī (m), schoolmaster,
   master
46 magistrátus, -ūs (m), magistrate

150

magníficus, -a, -um, magnificent

mágnus, -a, -um, great, big, large, loud (voice)

máior, -óris, greater

53 maióres, -um (m pl), ancestors

45 málō, -lle (irreg.), -luī, to prefer

málus, -a, -um, bad, evil

máne, early in the day, in the morning

máneō, -ére (2), -sī, -sum, to remain, stay

53 mánēs, -ium (m pl), spirits of the dead

47 mānsuétus, -a, -um, tame

mánus, -ūs (f), hand, band (of men)

máppa, -ae (f), napkin

52 marítus, -ī (m), husband

máter, -tris (f), mother

49 mātrimónium, -ī (n), marriage

49 in mātrimónium dúcere, to marry

51 mātróna, -ae (f), married woman

45 mātúrē, early

máximus, -a, -um, very great, greatest, very large

máximē, very much, very, most

mécum, with me

53 médicus, -ī (m), doctor

médius, -a, -um, mid-, middle of

Mehércule! By Hercules! Goodness me!

45 memorábilis, -is, -e, memorable

ménsa, -ae (f), table

ménsis, -is (m), month

mercátor, -óris (m), merchant

46 merīdiánī, -órum (m pl), midday fighters

44 merídiēs, -éī (m), noon, midday

53 méritum, -ī (n), good deed, (pl) services

53 mérita cōnférre, to render services (to)

métus, -ūs (m), fear

47 métū exanimátus, paralyzed with fear

méus, -a, -um, my, mine

44 mícō, -áre (1), -uī, to move quickly to and fro, flash

44 dígitīs micáre, to play morra

míles, -itis (m), soldier

mílle, a thousand

46 mília, thousands

mínimē, least, no

mínuō, -úere (3), -uī, -útum, to lessen, reduce, decrease

mínus, less

47 mīrábilis, -is, -e, wonderful

48 míror, -árī (1), -átus sum, to wonder

mírus, -a, -um, wonderful, marvelous, strange

míser, -era, -erum, unhappy, miserable, wretched

47 mítis, -is, -e, gentle

míttō, -ere (3), mísī, míssum, to send, let go

módo, only

módus, -ī (m), way, method

moléstus, -a, -um, troublesome, annoying

móneō (2), to advise, warn

53 monuméntum, -ī (n), monument, tomb

53 mórbus, -ī (m), illness

53 mórior, -ī (3), -tuus sum, to die

moror, -árī (1), -átus sum, to delay, remain, stay

mors, -tis (f), death

52 mortíferē, mortally, critically

mórtuus, -a, -um, dead

51 mōs, móris (m), custom

móveō, -ére (2), móvī, mótum, to move, shake

mox, soon, presently

mulíebris, -is, -e, womanly, female, of a woman

múlier, -eris (f), woman

multitúdō, -inis (f), crowd

	múltus, -a, -um, much, (*pl*) many
47	**múltō**, by much, much
	múltum (*adverb*), much, long
45	**múnus, -eris** (*n*), gladiatorial show, (*pl*) games
	múrus, -ī (*m*), wall
	mússō (1), to mutter
47	**mútuus, -a, -um**, mutual, common, of each other
52	**mýrtus, -ī** (*f*), myrtle

N

nam, for

nárrō (1), to tell (a story)

44 **nātális, -is, -e** (belonging to) birth

44 **díēs nātális**, birthday

nātúra, -ae (*f*), nature

53 **nātus (gnátus), -ī** (*m*), son

nāvigō (1), to sail

návis, -is (*f*), ship

-ne, (indicates a question)

50 **nē** (+ *subjunctive*), in case, to prevent, not to

nē . . . quídem, not even

51 **nē quis**, that no one

43 **nec**, and . . . not

nec . . . nec . . ., neither . . . nor

nécō (1), to kill

49 **néglegō, -gere** (3), **-xī, -ctum**, to neglect, ignore

45 **negōtiósus, -a, -um**, busy

némō, -inis (*m*), no one

53 **nénia, -ae** (*f*), lament, dirge

néque, and . . . not

néque . . . néque . . ., neither . . . nor . . .

41 **Nerōnéus, -a, -um**, of Nero

nésciō (4), to be ignorant, not know

níhil, nothing

níl, nothing

nísi, unless, if . . . not, except

49 **nóbilis, -is, -e**, noble

nócte, at night

43 **nóctū**, by night, at night

nólō, -lle, -luī, to be unwilling, not wish, refuse

nómen, -inis (*n*), name

nóminō (1), to name, call by name

nōn, not

nóndum, not yet

Nónne . . . ? (introduces a question that expects the answer "yes")

50 **nōnnúllī, -ae, -a**, some

nónus, -a, -um, ninth

nōs, we, us

nóster, -tra, -trum, our

nóvem, nine

nóvus, -a, -um, new

nox, -ctis (*f*), night

52 **núbō, -bere** (3), **-psī, -ptum** (+ *dat.*), to marry

núllus, -a, -um, no, none

44 **Num . . . ?** Surely . . . not . . . ? (introduces a question that expects the answer "no")

númerō (1), to count

númquam, never

nunc, now

núntius, -ī (*m*), messenger

49 **núper**, recently

52 **(nóva) núpta, -ae** (*f*), bride

52 **nūptiális, -is, -e**, wedding (adjective)

núsquam, nowhere

52 **nux, núcis** (*f*), nut

O

obdórmiō (4), to go to sleep

óbsecrō (1), to beseech, beg

49 **obsérvō** (1), to watch, pay attention to

52 **obsígnō** (1), to sign

46 **obstupefáctus, -a, -um**, astounded

occásiō, -ónis (*f*), opportunity

43 **occídō, -dere** (3), **-dī, -sum**, to kill

occupátus, -a, -um, busy

óctō, eight

óculus, -ī (m), eye
53 officiósus, -a, -um, ready to serve, obliging
50 officium, -ī (n), official ceremony, duty
ólim, once upon a time, one day
ómnis, -is, -e, all, the whole, every, each
ónerō (1), to load
52 opériō, -íre (4), -uī, -tum, to hide, cover
49 opórtet tē (+ infin.), you must
óptimus, -a, -um, best, very good, excellent
53 óptō (1), to wish
43 órior, -írī (4), -tus sum, to rise
ōrnáméntum, -ī (n), decoration
52 órnō (1), to decorate, equip
50 órō (1), to beg
43 ōs, óris (n), mouth, face, expression
os, óssis (n), bone
43 ósculum, -ī (n), kiss
46 osténdō, -dere (3), -dī, -tum, to show, point out

P

paedagógus, -ī (m), tutor
paéne, almost
41 palaéstra, -ae (f), exercise-ground
Palātínus, -a, -um, belonging to the Palatine Hill
41 pálus, -ī (m), post
pánis, -is (m), bread
44 pār ímpār, odds or evens (a game)
47 párcō, -cere (3), pepércī (+ dat.), to spare
párēns, -ntis (m/f), parent
páreō (2) (+ dat.), to obey
46 pária, -ium (n pl), pairs
párō (1), to prepare
pars, -tis (f), part
párvus, -a, -um, small
páter, -tris (m), father
51 pátrēs, -um (m pl), senators

pátior, -tī (3), -ssus sum, to suffer, endure
pátruus, -ī (m), uncle
paúcī, -ae, -a, few
paulátim, gradually, little by little
paulísper, for a short time
52 paúlō post, a little later
paúlum, a little, little
42 pavīméntum, -ī (n), tiled floor
53 péctus, -oris (n), chest, breast
53 péctus plángere, to beat the breast
pecúnia, -ae (f), money
per (+ acc.), through, along, over
43 pérdō, -ere (3), -idī, -itum, to destroy
51 pérferō, -rre (irreg.), pértulī, perlátum, to report
perículum, -ī (n), danger
44 peristýlium, -ī (n), peristyle, courtyard surrounded with a colonnade
53 pérlegō, -égere (3), -égī, -éctum, to read through
persuádeō, -dére (2), -sī, -sum (+ dat.), to persuade
pertérritus, -a, -um, frightened, terrified
49 perturbátus, -a, -um, confused
pervéniō, -eníre (4), -énī, -éntum (ad + acc.), to reach, arrive (at)
pēs, pédis (m), foot
péssimus, -a, -um, worst
pétō, -ere (3), -ívī, -ītum, to seek, aim at, attack
41 píla, -ae (f), ball
pīráta, -ae (m), pirate
53 pístor, -óris (m), baker
pláceō (2), (+ dat.), to please
47 plácidē, quietly, tamely
51 plácuit, it was decided
53 plángō, -gere (3), -xī, -ctum, to beat

153

53   péctus plángere, to beat the
       breast
       plḗnus, -a, -um, full
       plúit, -úere (3), plúit, it is raining
       plū́rimus, -a, -um, most, very
        much
       plūs, plū́ris, more
43   pollíceor, -érī (2), -itus sum, to
       promise
53   pómpa, -ae (f), funeral procession
       pốnō, pốnere (3), pósuī, pósitum,
       to put, place
       pópulus, -ī (m), people
       pórcus, -ī (m), pig
       pórta, -ae (f), gate
       pốrtō (1), to carry
       póscō, -ere (3), popóscī, to ask for,
       demand
       póssum, pósse (irreg.), pótuī, to be
       able
       post (adverb), after(wards), later
52   paúlō post, a little later
       post (+ acc.), after
41   pósteā, afterwards
51   pósterus, -a, -um, next, following
       póstis, -is (m), door-post
44   postrḗmō, finally
53   postrḗmus, -a, -um, last
       postrídiē, on the following day
51   pótius quam, rather than
51   praébeō (2), to display, show,
       provide
52   praecḗdō, -édere (3), -éssī, -éssum,
       to go in front
50   praecípiō, -ípere (3), -épī, -éptum
       (+ dat.), to instruct, order
       praeclā́rus, -a, -um, distinguished,
       famous
       praédō, -ốnis (m), robber
       praéter (+ acc.), except, beyond
       praetéreā, besides, moreover
       praetéxta (toga), with purple edge
51   praetextā́tus, -a, -um, wearing the
       toga praetexta

42   prehéndō, -dere (3), -dī, -sum, to
       seize
       prī́mus, -a, -um, first
       prī́ma lūx, dawn
       prī́mō, at first, first
       prī́mum (adverb), first
       prī́nceps, -cipis (m), emperor,
       leader, leading citizen
43   prī́or, -ốris, first (of two), previous
46   prī́us, previously
45   prō cértō hábeō, I am sure
       Prō dī immortā́lēs! Good heavens!
42   prōcḗdō, -dere (3), -ssī, -ssum, to
       step forward
       prócul, in the distance, far off
51   prốferō, -férre (irreg.), -tulī, -lā́tum,
       to carry forward, continue
       proficíscor, -icíscī (3), -éctus sum,
       to set out
       prōgrédior, -dī (3), -ssus sum, to go
       forward, advance
49   prốnuba, -ae (f), bride's attendant
43   própe (adverb), near, nearly
       própe (+ acc.), near
49   propī́nquus, -ī (m), relative
       própter (+ acc.), on account of
52   prōrúmpō, -úmpere (3), -úpī,
       -úptum, to burst forth, burst
       out
       prū́dēns, -ntis, wise, sensible
51   prūdéntia, -ae (f), good sense, dis-
       cretion, skill
50   pū́blicus, -a, -um, public
       puélla, -ae (f), girl
       púer, -erī (m), boy
50   puerī́lis, -is, -e, childish, of child-
       hood
46   púgna, -ae (f), battle
46   púgnam commíttere, to join
       battle
46   púgnō (1), to fight
       púlcher, -chra, -chrum, beautiful,
       handsome
52   pulchritū́dō, -inis (f), beauty

46 pulvínar, -áris (*n*), imperial seat (at games)

púniō (4), to punish

44 púpa, -ae (*f*), doll

púrus, -a, -um, spotless, clean, plain white

44 putō (1), to think, consider

Quómodo . . . ? How . . . ? In what way . . . ?

quóniam, since

quóque, also

Quot . . . ? How many . . . ?

Quótus, -a, -um . . . ? Which (in numerical order) . . . ?

Q

quaérō, -rere (3), -sívī, -sítum, to seek, look for, ask (for)

Quális . . . ? What sort of . . . ? In what state (or condition) . . . ?

Quam . . . ! How . . . !

quam, than

51 pótius quam, rather than

quam (+ *superlative*), as . . . as possible

quámquam, although

Quándō . . . ? When . . . ?

Quántus, -a, -um . . . ? How big . . . ? How much . . . ?

47 quási, as if

-que, and

quī, quae, quod, who, which, that

quídam, quaédam, quóddam, a certain, (*pl*) some

quídem, indeed

nē . . . quídem, not even

quiéscō, -ere (3), quiévī, quiétum, to rest, keep quiet

quínque, five

quíntus, -a, -um, fifth

Quis . . . ? Quid . . . ? Who . . . ? What . . . ? Which . . . ?

Quid agis? How are you?

50 (sī) quis (see aliquis)

51 (nē) quis (see aliquis)

41 quō, there, to that place

Quō . . . ? Where . . . to?

quō . . . eō . . . , the (more) . . . the (more)

quod, because

R

rápiō, -ere (3), -uī, -tum, to snatch, seize

rē vérā, really, actually

53 recípiō, -ípere (3), -épī, -éptum, to receive

47 recognítiō, -ónis (*f*), recognition

recúmbō, -mbere (3), -buī, to recline, lie down

réctē, rightly, properly

réddō, -ere (3), -idī, -itum, to give back, return

53 redémptor, -óris (*m*), contractor

rédeō, -íre (*irreg.*), -iī, -itum, to return, go back

redúcō, -cere (3), -xī, -ctum, to lead back, take back

44 réferō, -rre (*irreg.*), réttulī, relátum, to bring back

régnum, -ī (*n*), kingdom

regrédior, -dī (3), -ssus sum, to go back, return

relínquō, -ínquere (3), -íquī, -íctum, to leave

repéllō, -ere (3), réppulī, repúlsum, to drive off, drive back, beat back

41 répetō, -ere (3), -ívī, -ítum, to pick up, fetch, recover

reprehéndō, -dere (3), -dī, -sum, to blame, scold, reprimand

rēs, réī (*f*), thing, matter, affair, situation

rēs urbánae, affairs of the town

48 rē vérā, really, actually

155

49 rescríbō, -bere (3), -psī, -ptum, to
    write back, reply
46 reservātus, -a, -um, reserved
    resístō, -ístere (3), -titī (+ dat.), to
    resist
    respíciō, -ícere (3), -éxī, -éctum, to
    look back, look around at
    respóndeō, -dére (2), -dī, -sum, to
    answer, reply
    retíneō, -ére (2), -uī, retentum, to
    hold back, keep
48 rē vérā, really
    rídeō, -dére (2), -sī, -sum, to laugh,
    laugh at, smile
41 rīdículus, -a, -um, absurd, laugha-
    ble
43 ríma, -ae (f), crack
    rísus, -ūs (m), laughter, laugh,
    smile
52 ríte, properly
43 ríxor, -árī (1), -átus sum, to quarrel
    rógō (1), to ask
53 rógus, -ī (m), funeral pyre
    Róma, -ae (f), Rome
    Rōmánus, -a, -um, Roman
    rúrsus, again
    russátus, -a, -um, red
    rústicus, -a, -um, of or belonging to
    the country or farm

S
    sácer, -cra, -crum, sacred, religious,
    holy
52 sácra, -órum (n pl), sacrifice
52 sacríficō (1), to sacrifice
    saépe, often
43 saévus, -a, -um, fierce, savage
    salútō (1), to greet, welcome
    Sálvē! Salvéte! Greetings! Good
    morning! Hello!
43 sanguíneus, -a, -um, bloodstained
    sánguis, -inis (m), blood
    sátis, enough
    sceléstus, -a, -um, wicked

41 scélus, -eris (n), crime
    scíndō, -ere (3), scídī, scíssum, to
    cut, split, carve
53 scíssā véste, with torn clothing
    scíō (4), to know
    scríbō, -bere (3), -psī, -ptum, to
    write
    sē, himself, herself, oneself, itself,
    themselves
43 sēcrétō, secretly
    sécum, with him (her, it, them)
    (-self, -selves)
    sed, but
50 sédecim, sixteen
    sédeō, -ére (2), sédī, séssum, to sit
    sélla, -ae (f), sedan chair, seat,
    chair
    sémper, always
    senátor, -óris (m), senator
41 senátus, -ūs (m), senate
41 sénex, -is (m), old man
43 séntiō, -tíre (4), -sī, -sum, to feel,
    notice, realize
    sepéliō, -elíre (4), -elívī, -últum, to
    bury
    sepúlc(h)rum, -ī (n), tomb
    séquor, -quī (3), -útus sum, to
    follow
49 serénus, -a, -um, clear, bright
53 sérmo, -ónis (m), conversation, talk
    sérō, late
49 sérva, -ae (f), slave-woman, slave-
    girl
    sérvō (1), to save, keep, protect
    sérvus, -ī (m), slave
    sex, six
    séxtus, -a, -um, sixth
    sī, if
50 sī quis (= áliquis), if anyone
    sīc, thus, in this way
52 síccus, -a, -um, dry
    sígnum, -ī (n), signal, sign
    siléntium, -ī (n), silence
    sílva, -ae (f), woods

156

9 símilis, -is, -e (+ *dat.*), like, similar (to)

símul, together, at the same time

símulō (1), to pretend

síne (+ *abl.*), without

9 siníster, -tra, -trum, left

3 sítus, -a, -um, placed, buried

9 sōl, sólis (*m*), sun

sóleō, -ére (2), -itus sum, to be accustomed, in the habit

9 sōlitúdō, -inis (*f*), loneliness, solitude

sollícitus, -a, -um, anxious, worried

sólus, -a, -um, alone

sóror, -óris (*f*), sister

spectáculum, -ī (*n*), sight, spectacle

spectátor, -óris (*m*), spectator, onlooker

spéctō (1), to watch, look at

spéculum, -ī (*n*), mirror

3 spēlúnca, -ae (*f*), cave

5 spérō (1), to hope

9 spóndeō, -dére (2), spopóndī, -sum, to promise solemnly, pledge

9 spónsa, -ae (*f*), betrothed woman, bride

9 spōnsália, -ium (*n pl*), betrothal

9 spónsus, -ī (*m*), betrothed man, bridegroom

státim, immediately

7 stírps, -pis (*f*), thorn

stō, stáre (1), stétī, státum, to stand

strépitus, -ūs (*m*), noise, din, clattering

1 strígilis, -is (*f*), strigil, scraper

stríngō, -ngere (3), -nxī, -ctum, to draw (a sword)

stúltus, -a, -um, stupid, foolish

stúpeō (2), to be amazed, gape

sub (+ *abl.*), under, beneath

súbitō, suddenly

9 submíssus, -a, -um, quiet, subdued, soft

49 submíssā vōce, in a subdued voice

42 súbsequor, -quī (3), -cútus sum, to follow (up)

sum, ésse (*irreg.*), fúī, to be

súmmus, -a, -um, very great, the greatest, the top of . . .

súmō, -mere (3), -mpsī, -mptum, to take, pick out, pick up, assume, put on

súperō (1), to overcome, defeat

súrgo, -rgere (3), -rréxī, -rréctum, to get up, rise

42 surrípiō, -ípere (3), -ípuī, -éptum, to steal

súus, -a, -um, his, her, one's, its, their (-own)

T

tablínum, -ī (*n*), study (room)

50 tábulae, -árum (*f pl*), tablets, records

50 Tabulárium, -ī (*n*), Public Records Office

táceō (2), to be quiet

52 taéda, -ae (*f*), torch

49 taédet, it bores, makes one (*acc.*) tired of something (*gen.*)

49 mē taédet (+ *gen.*), I am bored (with), tired (of)

tális, -is, -e, such, of this kind

tam, so

támen, however, nevertheless

tándem, at last, at length

tántus, -a, -um, so great

49 tántum, so much

temerárius, -a, -um, rash, reckless, bold

tempéstās, -átis (*f*), storm

témplum, -ī (*n*), temple

témpus, -oris (*n*), time

téneō, -ére (2), -uī, -tum, to hold

41 tepidárium, -ī (*n*), warm room (at baths)

157

41 térgeō, -gére (2), -sī, -sum, to dry,
      wipe
    térra, -ae (f), earth
    térror, -óris (m), terror, fear
    tértius, -a, -um, third
46 téssera, -ae (f), ticket
41 thérmae, -árum (f pl), public baths
43 Thísbē, -ēs (f), Thisbe
48 tígris, -is (m/f), tiger
    tímeō (2), to fear
    tímidus, -a, -um, afraid, fearful,
      timid
43 tímidē, fearfully, timidly
    tímor, -óris (m), fear
    tóga, -ae (f), toga
    tóga praetéxta, toga with purple
      edging
50 tóga púra, plain white toga
    tóga virílis, toga worn by adult
      male (plain white)
46 tóllō, -ere (3), sústulī, sublátum, to
      lift, raise
46 tot, so many
    tótus, -a, -um, all, the whole
    trádō, -ere (3), -idī, -itum, to hand
      over
    tráhō, -here (3), -xī, -ctum, to drag,
      pull
    tránsgrédior, -dī (3), -ssus sum, to
      cross
    trémō, -ere (3), -uī, to tremble
51 trépidāns, -ntis, in a panic
    trēs, trēs, tría, three
41 trígōn, -ónis (m), ball game involv-
      ing three people
    trístis, -is, -e, sad
    tū, you (sing.)
46 túbicen, -inis (m), trumpet-player
    tum, at that moment, then
    tumúltus, -ūs (m), uproar, din,
      commotion
    túnica, -ae (f), tunic
    túrba, -ae (f), crowd
    túus, -a, -um, your (sing.)

U
Úbi . . . ? Where . . . ?
úbi, where, when
úlulō (1), to howl
úmbra, -ae (f), shadow, shade (of
  the dead)
úmquam, ever
únā, together
Únde . . . ? Where . . . from?
úndique, on all sides, from all sides
41 unguéntum, -ī (n), ointment, per-
      fume, oil
41 únguō, -guere (3), -xī, -ctum, to
      anoint, smear with oil
    únus, -a, -um, one
    urbánus, -a, -um, of the city or
      town
    rēs urbánae, affairs of the town
    urbs, -bis (f), city
51 úrgeō, -ére (2), úrsī, to press, insist
    ut (+ indicative), when, as
49 ut (+ subjunctive), so that, that, to
43 utérque, útraque, utrúmque, each
      (of two), both
51 útrum . . . an . . . ,
      whether . . . or . . .
    úxor, -óris (f), wife

V
váldē, very, very much
Válē! Valéte! Goodbye!
43 valedícō, -cere (3), -xī, -ctum, to
      say goodbye, bid farewell
41 vápor, -óris (m), steam
41 várius, -a, -um, different, various,
      varied
    veheménter, violently, furiously,
      insistently
    vel, or
    vel . . . vel . . . ,
      either . . . or . . .
43 vēlámen, -inis (n), veil, shawl,
      head-scarf

158

vēnátiō, -ónis (f), hunting, animal hunt

véndō, -ere (3), -idī, -itum, to sell

véniō, veníre (4), vénī, véntum, to come

véntus, -ī (m), wind

vérberō (1), to beat

verbósus, -a, -um, talkative   53

vérbum, -ī (n), word, verb

véreor, -érī (1), -itus sum, to be   43
afraid, fear

vérus, -a, -um, true
rē vérā, really, actually
vérō, truly, really, actually   53
Íta vérō! Yes!   52

véscor, -ī (3) (+ abl.), to feed (on)   43

véster, -tra, -trum, your (pl.)

vestíbulum, -ī (n), entrance passage

vestígium, -ī (n), track, footprint, trace

vestīménta, -órum (n pl), clothes

véstis, -is (f), clothing, garment
scíssā véste, with torn clothing

vétō, -áre (1), -uī, -itum, to forbid,   49
tell not to

véxō (1), to annoy, tease

vía, -ae (f), road, street

viátor, -óris (m), traveler   43

vīcínus, -a, -um, neighboring   49

vídeō, vidére (2), vídī, vísum, to see

vídeor, vidérī (2), vísus sum, to seem, be seen

vílla, -ae (f), farmhouse

víncō, -ere (3), vícī, víctum, to win, conquer, overcome

vínum, -ī (n), wine

víolō (1), to do harm to

vir, vírī (m), man

vírgō, -inis (f), maiden

virílis, -is, -e, a man's, of a man

vīs, vim (acc.), vī (abl.) (f), force

vísitō (1), to visit

víta, -ae (f), life

vítta, -ae (f), ribbon, headband

vívō, -vere (3), -xī, -ctum, to live

vix, scarcely, with difficulty, only just

vócō (1), to call, invite

vólō, vélle (irreg.), vóluī, to wish, want, be willing

vōs, you (pl.)

vōx, vócis (f), voice
submíssā vóce, in a subdued voice

vúlnerō (1), to wound

vúlnus, -eris (n), wound

vúltus, -ūs (f), face, expression
vúltū dēmíssō, with eyes lowered

159

ACKNOWLEDGMENTS

For providing us with photographs, drawings or permission to publish extracts from their publications, we would like to thank:

Page 9: Reproduced by Courtesy of the Trustees of the British Museum, photograph of a bronze oil flask and two strigils. Page 12: The Mansell Collection, photograph of the women's changing room. Page 13: Reprinted by the publisher, George Braziller, Inc., drawing of Hadrian's Baths at Lepcis Magna. Page 16: The Mansell Collection, photograph of Baths of Caracalla. Page 38: Scala/Art Resource, NY, photograph of women playing knucklebones. Page 46: Photograph, Peter Clayton, photograph of the Colosseum. Page 51: The Trustees of the British Museum, photograph of a sestertius. Page 58: The Mansell Collection, a drawing of a sea fight. Page 63: The Mansell Collection, photograph of a gladiator's helmet. Page 81: The Trustees of the British Museum, photograph of a betrothal ring. Pages 88–89: The Mansell Collection, photograph of a procession on its way to the altar. Page 106: Claudia Karabaic Sargent, drawing of statue of a man carrying funeral busts. Page 108: Claudia Karabaic Sargent, drawing of funeral relief.

The extract on page 21: From *The Satyricon* by Petronius, translated by William Arrowsmith. Copyright © 1959 by William Arrowsmith. Reprinted by arrangement with New American Library, New York, New York.

The extract on page 57: *Roman Voices: Everyday Latin in Ancient Rome* by Carol Clemeau Esler and *Teacher's Guide to Roman Voices: Everyday Latin in Ancient Rome*, published by Gilbert Lawall, 71 Sand Hill Road, Amherst, MA 01002.

The extracts on the following pages are reprinted by permission of Harvard University Press and The Loeb Classical Library, Cambridge, Mass.:

Page 21: *Plautus*, Volume IV, translated by Paul Nixon, (1965).

Page 26: *Satires, Epistles, and Ars Poetica* by Horace, translated by H. Rushton Fairclough, (1978).

Page 38–39: *The Art of Love, and Other Poems* by Ovid, translated by J. H. Mozley, (1962).

Page 39: *De Officiis*, Volume XXI by Cicero, translated by Walter Miller, (1975).

Page 39: *Suetonius*, Volume I, translated by J. C. Rolfe, (1979).

Page 40: *Moral Essays*, Volume II by Seneca, translated by John W. Basore, (1965).

Page 48: *Martial Epigrams*, Volume I, translated by Walter C. A. Ker, (1979).

Page 66: *Ad Lucilium Epistulae Morales*, Volume I by Seneca, translated by Richard M. Gummere, (1967).

Page 81: *The Attic Nights of Aulus Gellius*, Volume II, translated by John C. Rolfe, (1982).

Page 87: *Letters of Atticus*, Volume I by Cicero, translated by E. O. Winstedt, (1962).

Page 87: *Letters of Atticus*, Volume II by Cicero, translated by E. O. Winstedt, (1966).

Page 90: *Livy*, Volume I, translated by B. O. Foster, (1957).

Page 90: *De Senectute, De Amicitia, De Diviniatione*, Volume XX by Cicero, translated by William Armistead Falconer, (1979).

Page 102: *Pliny the Younger: Letters and Panegyricus*, Volume I, translated by Betty Radice, (1969).